DATE DUE

MAR 27 1995	
MAR 12 1997	

BRODART   Cat. No. 23-221

THE IMAGINATION OF DISASTER

THE
IMAGINATION
OF DISASTER

Evil in the Fiction of Henry James

BY J. A. WARD

University of Nebraska Press
Lincoln   1961

The publication of this book was assisted by a grant from the Ford Foundation.

Publishers on the Plains

UNP

for
ANN

Preface

The purpose of this book is to investigate what seems to me a major yet relatively neglected aspect of James's fiction. It has often been remarked that evil in James usually takes the form of what Hawthorne in "Ethan Brand" calls the "Unpardonable Sin," the malign intervention of one person in the life of another; but there has been no systematic consideration of the forms and implications of this evil or of its relevance to James's general fictional purposes. Likewise, several critics have observed—but usually in other connections—that in the development from the early to the late fiction, the words "villain" and "hero" become increasingly less applicable to James's characters. One of my intentions is to reveal the changes and patterns in James's characterizations of the evildoer, and thus to shed light on a subject that has been illuminated only in part.

My emphasis is literary rather than theological or moral. The subject "evil" is a means to an end; it serves as a new focus for an explication of James's fiction. Therefore I do not concern myself with evil as such; and the definition of evil which I presuppose throughout is intentionally broad, so as to protect me from any arbitrary limitation of subject matter. Paul Siwek, a Jesuit, in *The Philosophy of Evil* provides the most inclusive and succinct definition of evil that I have seen:

> [Evil is] all that opposes the intrinsic finality of a being. Therefore it is all that hinders the being's full development, all that thwarts its tendencies, all that resists the drive from the depths of that being toward full expansion, toward that completion which it would attain to in its ideal type, the archetype of its own nature (p. 50).

This definition is more satisfactory, because more philosophical, than those which define evil as that which destroys or which causes suffering. Furthermore, it crosses over a number of philosophical and theological boundaries, because, at least out of context, it leaves open the question of what "full expansion" is, and does not specify "all that opposes . . . finality."

However, with the implicit identification of good with growth, the definition seems especially useful for the consideration of a writer fundamentally in the tradition of nineteenth-century romanticism. For James, as for Wordsworth, Shelley, Emerson, and Thoreau, good is constant, unending development, and evil is stasis, or restriction of development. Growth in James's fiction is not nearly so natural as in a writer like Whitman: development for James requires a delicate balance between self and society, not a rejection of human institutions in the name of freedom or self-expression. In the main, evil in James is the complex of forces, internal and external, which prevents the individual from moving toward completion, always moral and spiritual, and sometimes intellectual, emotional, and aesthetic, toward which his nature strives.

This book is in no way intended to be a complete account of James's productions, although most of the major novels are discussed and some of the minor ones are treated rather extensively. The plays have been excluded because, though they are useful for a study of James's fictional technique, they at best only parallel and at worst soften the moral issues of the fiction. As Leon Edel makes clear in his introduction and notes to *The Complete Plays of Henry James*, the plays have an obviousness and conventionality seldom present in James's fiction.

After an introductory chapter dealing with general characteristics of James's treatment of evil, the subsequent chapters attempt to apply these generalizations successively to the four major divisions of James's writing: the early international fiction (1870–1889); the English, or "middle period," fiction (1890–1901); the later international fiction, that of the "major phase" (1902–1904); and the scattered fiction of James's last years (1905–1916). In spite of its obvious limitations, this scheme has seemed the most workable for the purposes of this study. For example, *The Bostonians*, set entirely in America, is treated under the general heading of the international theme, because this novel offers a revelation of James's critical attitude toward America which does much to clarify the moral opposition of America and Europe. The order is only generally chronological; within each of the four main divisions the order followed is that which seems most appropriate to the topic.

Acknowledgments

In the course of writing and rewriting this book, I have received much valuable assistance and advice. I especially wish to acknowledge the wisdom, generosity, and patience of Professor Richard Harter Fogle of Tulane University, who first encouraged me to deal with the subject, guided my work to completion in its first form as a doctoral dissertation, and carefully read the revised version I prepared for publication. Professors Richard P. Adams, John D. Husband, and George W. Meyer of Tulane, Professor Richard T. Wagner of the University of Southwestern Louisiana, and Professor B. R. McElderry, Jr. of the University of Southern California have also read the manuscript in entirety; to each of these I am very grateful. The notes suggest the extent of my indebtedness to all the critics and scholars whose work has helped my understanding of James.

I also wish to thank the editors and directors of the following journals and presses for permission to reprint portions of this study which first appeared in article form: *Twentieth Century Literature* for "Henry James and the Nature of Evil," slightly enlarged as Chapter One; *Mississippi Quarterly* for "Henry James's America: Versions of Oppression," slightly altered as part one of Chapter Two; *Texas Studies in Literature and Language* for "The Ineffectual Heroes of James's Middle Period," slightly enlarged as part one of Chapter Three; *Arizona Quarterly* for "Social Criticism in James's London Fiction," slightly altered as part two of Chapter Three; The Regents of the University of California and the University of California Press, publishers of *Nineteenth-Century Fiction,* for "*The Ambassadors:* Strether's Vision of Evil," © 1959 by The Regents, slightly enlarged as part one of Chapter Three; the Wayne State University Press, publishers of *Criticism,* for "Social Disintegration in *The Wings of the Dove,*" copyright 1960 by Wayne State University Press, slightly enlarged as part two of Chapter Four; and the *Western Humanities Review* for "Evil in *The Golden Bowl,*" slightly altered as part three of Chapter Four.

I am indebted to the following publishers for permission to quote from materials on which they hold copyright: to the American Book Company, for a quotation from the introduction to *Henry James: Representative Selections,* by Lyon N. Richardson; to E. P. Dutton & Co., Inc., publishers of *The Pilgrimage of Henry James,* by Van Wyck Brooks; to George W. Stewart, publisher of *The Great Tradition* by F. R. Leavis; to Grove Press, Inc., for permission to

ix

quote from *The Sacred Fount* by Henry James and the Introduction to *The Golden Bowl* by R. P. Blackmur; to Harper & Brothers, publishers of *The Wind Blew from the East* by Ferner Nuhn; to Holt, Rinehart and Winston, Inc., publishers of *The Question of Henry James: A Collection of Critical Essays*, edited by F. W. Dupee; to the Houghton Mifflin Company, publishers of *The Question of Our Speech and The Lesson of Balzac* by Henry James and *Henry James: Man and Author* by Pelham Edgar; to the *Journal of Aesthetics and Art Criticism*, for permission to quote from "The Relativism of Henry James" by Joseph J. Firebaugh; to the *Kenyon Review*, for permission to quote from "The Sacred Fount" by R. P. Blackmur and "Myth and Dialectic in the Later Novels" by Austin Warren; to the J. B. Lippincott Company, publishers of *Henry James: The Untried Years* by Leon Edel; to The Macmillan Company, publishers of *The Crooked Corridor: A Study of Henry James* by Elizabeth Stevenson and *The American Novel: 1789–1939* by Carl Van Doren; to *The New Republic*, for permission to quote from "The Choice So Freely Made," by Leon Edel; to the Oxford University Press, publishers of *Henry James: The Major Phase* by F. O. Matthiessen and *The Notebooks of Henry James;* to Paul R. Reynolds & Son, representative of the Henry James estate, for permission to quote from the volumes of *The Novels and Tales of Henry James* which it controls and for Canadian distribution rights; to Charles Scribner's Sons, publishers of *The Novels and Tales of Henry James, A Small Boy and Others, Notes of a Son and Brother, The Art of the Novel: Critical Prefaces by Henry James*, edited by Richard P. Blackmur, and *The Letters of Henry James*, edited by Percy Lubbock; to *The Sewanee Review*, for permission to quote from "*The Golden Bowl* Revisited" by Francis Fergusson; to the University of Chicago Press, publishers of *The American Adam* by R. W. B. Lewis, © 1955 by the University of Chicago; to the *University of Kansas City Review*, for permission to quote from "*The Turn of the Screw* as Poem" by Robert B. Heilman; to The Modern Language Association of America, publishers of *PMLA*, for permission to quote from "Henry James's World of Images" by R. W. Short; to the Ronald Press Company, publishers of *The Philosophy of Evil* by Paul Siwek, copyright 1951 by The Ronald Press Company; to The Viking Press, Inc., publishers of *Craft and Character in Modern Fiction* by Morton Dauwen Zabel; and to William Sloane Associates, Inc., publishers of *Henry James* by F. W. Dupee, copyright 1951 by William Sloane Associates, Inc.

Finally, I wish to express my thanks to the Ford Foundation, whose grant made possible the publication of this book.

Contents

THE IMAGINATION OF DISASTER

CHAPTER ONE

The Consciousness of Evil

HENRY JAMES is a realist in fiction, one who conceives of his art as an end, not as a means, and whose effort is to dramatize life, to depict life, and to give form to life, not to present a religious or philosophic system. Evil is present in his fiction as it is embodied in concrete characters and situations and as the characters reflect upon these. James's concern with evil is a concern with an aspect of reality, and therefore it is dealt with imaginatively rather than theologically or moralistically.

It is a testimony to James's consistent artistic development that there is in his works a distinct movement toward detachment in his treatment of evil. Just as the villains of his early stories are simply conceived, so his own condemnation of them is unequivocal. In "Madame de Mauves" (1874), for example, James employs an almost primitive imagery of black and white to convey moral values. Likewise his admiration for the heroine, Euphemia Cleve, whose unflinching righteousness offends the modern reader, and his disapproval of the duplicity and adultery of Richard de Mauves, establish an absolute moral dualism (possibly qualified by the ambiguous ending of the story) that is characteristic of many of James's early pieces. In his more mature stories of the early period, however, James maintains a disinterested position through an ironic approach to his heroes and heroines: Christopher Newman and Isabel Archer meet evil through weakness of character as well as through unfortunate circumstances. James achieves full detachment in his middle period when he replaces the stage villainy of the Bellegardes and Osmond with the ambiguous characterizations of Mrs. Gereth, Rose Armiger, and Mrs. Brookenham.

The Other House (1896) reveals the shift in James's view of

evil; it is the novel in which James continues to convey the horror
of evil, and yet divests the evildoer of the simple blackness that
often takes the place of realistic characterization in the early
works. *The Other House* is especially notable and unusual in that
it is about a crime of violence—specifically, the murder of a child.
Yet the villainess, Rose Armiger, is a subtle creation, looking forward to the ambiguous "bad heroines" of later works, especially
Kate Croy. Her evil is tempered and thus made credible by certain admirable traits. Rose's tremendous passion and vitality, her
grace and style are inseparable from her cruelty. James treats
Rose's evil as a psychologist rather than a moralist, and in doing so
makes her heinous crime believable.

The objective dramatic form of *The Other House* serves James
in his realism, but the toleration and qualified admiration for the
evildoer carry over to the last novels, which are subjective rather
than objective in approach. The later versions of the European
villain—Mme. de Vionnet, Kate Croy, and Prince Amerigo—bear
little resemblance to the earlier versions—Richard de Mauves,
Urbain de Bellegarde, and Gilbert Osmond. Moral conflict, however, becomes no less significant in the later works, but James's
ambiguity, complexity, and detachment prohibit critical literalism
and moralism.

In 1876, James wrote of Baudelaire that

> He knew evil not by experience, not as something within
> himself, but by contemplation and curiosity, as something
> outside of himself, by which his own intellectual agility was
> not in the least discomposed, rather indeed . . . flattered and
> stimulated. . . . evil for him begins outside and not inside,
> and consists primarily of a great deal of lurid landscape and
> unclean furniture. . . . Evil is represented as an affair of
> blood and carrion and physical sickness—there must be stink-
> ing corpses and starving prostitutes and empty laudanum
> bottles in order that the poet shall be effectively inspired.
> . . . he was, in his treatment of evil, exactly what Haw-
> thorne was not—Hawthorne, who felt the thing at its source,
> deep in the human consciousness.[1]

It is important to establish that for James evil resides primarily ✓ inside the human consciousness, for except in the background of his early fiction and in the foreground of *The Other House* there is little of stock horror and villainy in James's work. Stuart P. Sherman, accustomed to conventional nineteenth-century fictional techniques, accuses James of replacing genuine evil by bad manners: "[James's] controlling principle is a sense of style, under which vice, to adapt Burke's words, loses half its evil by losing all its grossness." [2] But in his critique of Baudelaire James makes explicit what is implicit in his fiction, his belief that the literary artist should deal with the evil which exists "deep in human consciousness." Though James gives evil external form, it originates in the will or the intellect and reveals its force by causing suffering that is not physical but emotional and mental. Moreover, evil partakes of the forms of civilization. It is detectable in the motives which bring it about and in the suffering which it causes, but in itself it may seem hardly significant or even nonexistent. One cannot accuse Dr. Sloper, Mme. Merle, or Christina Light of criminal action or even of conduct intrinsically reprehensible: our judgment of these and other "villains" must be based on their motivations and on the anguish they cause others.

Evil in James's fiction is not so much a problem as it is an inexorable, ever-present reality that cripples and destroys; it is present at the base of every human situation, and it is at least latent in every man. Critics frequently describe James as having a "sense of evil" (rather than an "idea of evil" or a "concept of evil"); and the term is accurate, for it suggests that to James evil is obscure and indefinite. In his works the reaction to evil often strikes us as vague and unrelated to specific action or character, or we may feel, as does Yvor Winters toward some of the novels, that the sense of evil far outweighs what the presented facts merit.[3] This sense of evil in James, this "imagination . . . clouded by the Pit," as Graham Greene terms it,[4] is based on or is equivalent to an imaginative recognition of a sin that, if it is not "original," is certainly fundamental to the human situation. James once wrote, ". . . I have the imagination of disaster and see life indeed ✓ as ferocious and sinister." [5] To R. P. Blackmur his fiction conveys "the menace of life itself." [6] A stoic who rejected the easy solutions of the optimist, James unquestionably shared the feeling of Mr. Vetch of *The Princess Casamassima:*

> The idea of great changes . . . took its place among the dreams of his youth; for what was any possible change in the relations of men and women but a new combination of the same elements? If the elements could be made different the thing would be worth thinking of; but it was not only impossible to introduce any new ones—no means had yet been discovered for getting rid of the old. The figures on the chessboard were still the passions and jealousies and superstitions and stupidities of man, and their position with regard to each other at any given moment could be of interest only to the grim invisible fates who played the game—who sat, through the ages, low-backed over the table (VI, 104).[7]

Significantly, James found one of Emerson's limitations to be his "ripe unconsciousness of evil"; [8] similarly he thought Hawthorne "most creative" when he showed "that we are really not by any means so good as a well-regulated society requires us to appear." [9] In one of his most profound letters he advised Grace Norton to "content yourself with the terrible algebra of your own [life]." [10] He considered his father's theological system invalidated by an "optimism fed so little by any sense of things as they were or are." [11] Probably James's most explicit comment on evil occurs in his essay on Turgenev: "Life *is,* in fact, a battle. On this point optimists and pessimists agree. Evil is insolent and strong; beauty enchanting but rare; goodness very apt to be weak; folly very apt to be defiant; wickedness to carry the day; imbeciles to be in great places, people of sense in small, and mankind generally, unhappy." [12]

James's acceptance, imaginative rather than literal, of "some terrible aboriginal catastrophe," to use Newman's phrase,[13] that made evil, if not a natural element of human life, certainly a permanent reality, takes the form in his novels of what theologians term "sin" rather than of what they term "evil," or of "moral evil" rather than "natural evil." Natural evil, which is beyond the realm of human control, the caprices and cataclysms of nature,

the unavoidable facts of disease and death, is, according to Rein-
hold Niebuhr, "an irrelevance and a threat of meaninglessness in
the realm of human history." [14] In James the emphasis on natural
evil is equally slight. It is of course an accepted reality, and
instances of it set many of his stories in motion: the illness and
death of Ralph Touchett and Milly Theale and such circumstan-
tial misfortunes as the poverty of Kate Croy and Merton Densher
are central to James's plots. But such matters are never treated for
their own value; they merely serve as bases for stories which have
moral evil at their center. James has so little concern for natural
evil that he very often makes death the result of moral rather than
of natural evil—as in *The Wings of the Dove*, "The Author of
Beltraffio," and "The Death of the Lion," in which the deaths
through natural causes of Milly Theale, Mark Ambient, and Neil
Paraday symbolize the spiritual suffering caused by unwarranted
human intervention. Other deaths, like those of May Bartram in
"The Beast in the Jungle" and Miss Pynsent in *The Princess
Casamassima*, are of little emotional or thematic value in themselves; they are necessary simply to accentuate moral situations.
May Bartram's death causes John Marcher to realize that his life
has been a spiritual death; the death of Miss Pynsent makes it
possible for Hyacinth Robinson to visit the continent and thereby
gain new awareness.[15]

In James's fiction man is not in a condition of absolute depravity, but he possesses a latent capacity for evil that is dreadful even
when unrealized. Perhaps central to James's treatment of evil is
this pervasive awareness of "the sin that dwelleth within me," the
strange and horrible existence of latent sin. James rarely treats this
sense of potential personal evil in his fiction directly, but it lies at
the center of many of his ghost stories, in which the ghosts are
"manifestations of a darker power inherent in the order of
things";[16] or, as R. P. Blackmur states, ". . . James's ghosts represent the attempt to give objective rational form—knowledge-
able form—to all the vast subjective experience of our 'other,' our
hidden, our secret selves which we commonly deny, gloss over, or
try to explain away."[17]

The central passage in James's work suggesting his consciousness of hidden personal evil is contained in his autobiographical
volume *A Small Boy and Others*, in which he describes

> the most appalling yet most admirable nightmare of my life.
> The climax of this extraordinary experience . . . was the
> sudden pursuit, through an open door, along a huge saloon,
> of a just dimly-descried figure that retreated in terror before
> my rush and dash (a glare of inspired reaction from irresisti-
> ble but shameful dread,) out of the room I had a moment
> before been desperately, and all the more abjectly, defending
> by the push of my shoulder against hard pressure on lock and
> bar from the other side. The lucidity, not to say the sub-
> limity, of the crisis had consisted of the great thought that I,
> in my appalled state, was probably still more appalling than
> the awful agent, creature or presence, whatever he was,
> whom I had guessed, in the suddenest wild start from sleep,
> the sleep within my sleep, to be making for my place of
> rest.[18]

The pattern of the terrified person finding himself even more
terrifying than the hideous monster who confronts him is a buried
motif in much of James's fiction, especially the late works. For
example, in *The Ambassadors* Strether's confrontation of Chad is
a case in which the appalled person is ultimately revealed as "still
more appalling than the awful agent." In *The Ambassadors*
Strether carries with him the evil of the New England conscience;
in *The Awkward Age* the character paralleling James in his
nightmare is Vanderbank, whose sin is pride: in each case, and in
many others, the character who in the beginning seems the victim
emerges as the source of evil.

James regularly makes evil latent and unconscious of itself.
It is often a power beyond will, beyond knowledge, beyond
identity. It is this obscure and irrational quality in his sense of evil
that links James to modern novelists like Kafka, whose Joseph K.
is on trial for an unnamed, unknown crime of which he yet is
guilty. It also links him to the diarists of the Puritan theocracy,
who relentlessly reflected on their own sins, and to Hawthorne,
many of whose characters were obsessed by their own guilt.

A resemblance that James noted between Hawthorne and the Puritans also holds true for his own fiction: "To him as to them, the consciousness of *sin* was the most importunate fact of life." [19] Evil in James is rarely isolated from the personal consciousness of it: either the subjective response of the disinterested observer (as in "The Two Faces," in which the cruel treatment of a girl by a jealous woman is not seen directly, but through the consciousness of a spectator, whose revulsion from the woman's behavior establishes the moral tone of the story), the consciousness of the guilty person (as in "Mora Montravers," in which the scornful uncle who abuses the innocent Mora is the reflector of the action), or the consciousness of the victim (as in *The American,* in which Christopher Newman suffers the effect of the villainy of the Bellegarde family).

Though James seems to be in the Puritan tradition in his subjective treatment of evil, there are some important modifications, alterations, and changes in emphasis in his works. James tends to concentrate on the good man's reaction to evil, rather than on the guilty man's obsession with his own sin. Thus the vision of evil in James more often resembles that of, say, Hilda in Hawthorne's *The Marble Faun,* the innocent made aware of evil, than it resembles the concern of Miriam with her own guilt. When James allows the reader to see into the mind of a villain, his emphasis differs from Hawthorne's. He is little interested in the sinner's sense of morality or in his feelings of guilt after the sin. Like most of the villains, the Bellegardes in *The American* and Gilbert Osmond in *The Portrait of a Lady* are never dealt with subjectively. We are permitted to see into the mind of Kate Croy, the instigator of the plot against Milly Theale in *The Wings of the Dove,* but we find no concern with sin or guilt. We perceive the subjective moral condition of Merton Densher, her accomplice, only when he regains the will to assert his temporarily suppressed sense of decency. In *The Golden Bowl* neither Charlotte Stant (whose mind we are not allowed to enter) nor Prince Amerigo seems conscious of his guilt. Nor is there any apparent struggle between will and conscience in these characters; the perpetrators of the evil cease their disruptive affair not because, like Arthur Dimmesdale of *The Scarlet Letter,* they are too burdened by

conscience to continue, but simply because they are defeated by
Maggie Verver.

The evil character in James is almost never reflective. The
characters who fully understand a situation are reduced to inactivity because of their knowledge. This knowledge is mainly a
moral awareness that enables the perceiver to grasp the full implications of a situation and thus to recognize the moral limitations
of any sort of private action. In this respect James is an Aristote-
lian: to him the will is subservient to the intellect; behavior and
thought must be in accordance. Nearly all the James characters
who have achieved total moral awareness are markedly passive;
their sole action is to accept their conditions. They renounce
escape, revenge, marriage, or any other course of action which
would relieve pain or improve their situations. The less perceptive
characters, on the other hand, are limited to a selfish view of life,
and as a result their wills control them. As James says of "the
awful Mona Brigstock" of *The Spoils of Poynton*, she "is *all* will,
without the smallest leak of force into taste or tenderness or
vision, into any sense of shades or relations or proportions." [20] In
James's fiction it is nearly axiomatic that the good are reflective
and passive, and the evil irreflective and active.

Though his villains are usually active, evil to James is a negative
reality. In this respect James, more in the tradition of Emerson
than that of Hawthorne and Melville, deviates from the modified
Manicheanism prevalent in much of American literature. In
James's fiction evil is not an active principle in the universe;
there are no Chillingworths or Ethan Brands, no Babos or Clag-
garts; there is no "evil according to nature" and no devotion to
evil for its own sake. The James character who injures others does
so through pursuit of good. James does not characterize pure
egotism, as does Hawthorne; rather he delineates characters
whose perception is limited—to art, as with Osmond; to social
decorum, as with Mme. Merle; to material goods, as with Mona
Brigstock; or to physical passion, as with Ida Farange. Evil comes
about through the imperception of those who either do not
recognize or ignore the effects of their activity on others. Thus
Osmond's devotion to aesthetics, in itself a good, brings misery
to his wife.

Furthermore, evil in James does not exist beyond human relationships. Occasionally melodramatic techniques lead James to
invest a particular family or civilization with a pervasive miasma,
suggestive of ineradicable evil; but in these cases theme and
setting conflict. The house of Pyncheon and the house of Usher
symbolize hereditary evil inevitably destroying each member of
the family. Unlike Hawthorne or Poe, however, James does not
treat evil beyond the level of psychology. Even in *The American*,
James's most melodramatic novel, hereditary evil operates merely
as an inclination, not a compulsion, which can be rejected by each
family member.

James follows the melodramatic, though not strictly Mani-
chean, convention of dramatizing conflicts between good and
evil. The Jamesian innocent, an embodiment of the principles of
Emersonian transcendentalism, cannot be identified with a total
goodness, but he represents an ultimate moral achievement.[21]
"Life [for James] was good and it was evil," writes Leon Edel;
"people were innocent, sometimes *bon enfant* and good natured,
or, on the other hand, predatory and destructive." [22] If the good
characters reflect a high view of human nature, we are never
allowed to forget that they form only part of the total picture and
that experience necessitates the encounter with evil, the supreme
test of the good nature.

Evil in James's world is ubiquitous only in the sense that it is
latent in every man. Nevertheless, it is unavoidable; it derives
from the fundamental human condition of limited perception.
Thus evil has its source in a part of existence more permanent and
essential than the vice of individuals.[23] It is not merely accidental
that Isabel Archer encounters Mme. Merle and that Milly Theale
becomes acquainted with Kate Croy. James's adventurers are
doomed from the beginning, because of the nature of the world
in which they live, to meet and be defeated by the force of evil.

Therefore, if the heroes and heroines are good, they rarely
achieve happiness or success. Often the complexity of life itself
is the villain, but evil is most often revealed in the stupidity, the
self-righteousness, or the rapacity of an individual or of a
society. Evil is unavoidable and universal, but it is centered in the
human soul and manifests itself in the harmful domination of one

person over another. Many James critics [24] have observed that the
principal sin in James is "[the violation of] the sanctity of the
human heart." [25] This element of personal violation, which has
been described as "emotional cannibalism" [26] and by James himself as "omnivorous egotism," [27] is James's version of Hawthorne's "Unpardonable Sin" and the major evil in his works.
James's inclination to associate egotism with imperception is not
shared by Hawthorne, but the effects of egotism are the same in
both authors—an emotional and spiritual crippling of the victim.

Though the resemblance between the treatments of sin by
Hawthorne and James is striking, James did much to alter both
the appearance and the activity of Hawthorne's villains. Especially in James's later works, in which the evildoer loses his
conventionally melodramatic features, his villains are lifelike,
whereas Hawthorne's rarely have an air of actuality; they
are embodiments of a principle of evil. Even in such early works
of James as *Roderick Hudson* and *The American,* the reprehensible characters, Mrs. Light and Urbain de Bellegarde, are motivated by common human desires—pride, greed, and revenge.
Such Hawthorne villains as Roger Chillingworth and Judge Pyncheon are Satan figures; they personify evil. As James is usually
more successful in giving solidity to his villains and their villainy,
he also attempts to translate the "Unpardonable Sin" into natural human action,[28] so that the villainy is not remote and vague,
but familiar and specific. In James the "Unpardonable Sin" is both
embodied in and indistinguishable from concrete human action,
such as adultery or theft or duplicity.[29]

James describes many kinds of personal violation, which are the
same in essence and effect but different in type. The victimizer
may be a false set of social values, as in many of the international
stories: Daisy Miller is destroyed by the artificial mores of a
decadent society. In most cases the sin takes the form of a person
or group of persons improperly using another individual: Maisie
Farange is little more than a pawn in the hands of her corrupt
elders as they use her to their own advantages.

James inevitably compounds the sin of personal violation by
associating it with betrayal. Gilbert Osmond, Paul Muniment,
Rose Armiger, Kate Croy, and nearly all the malefactors in James

are Judas-like in exploiting and destroying those whose confidence they have gained. Improper intervention in the life of another is virtually the only sin that interested James. Specific human actions, considered in isolation from other matters, are never in themselves evil (in this respect James is a moral relativist); the only criterion is the injury of another person. But in James's world of complex social relationships, human action does not take place in a vacuum, and the choice of one person inevitably results in either good or evil for others. Thus, deception (like that of Kate Croy and Merton Densher in *The Wings of the Dove*), theft (like that of Haughty Vint in *The Ivory Tower*), and adultery (like that of Beale Farange in *What Maisie Knew*) take their human tolls.

It is unnecessary to catalogue all the forms that personal violation assumes in James's fiction; in later chapters consideration is given to James's treatment of the common sins of pride, greed, and lust, and to the less common sin of ignorance. It is appropriate, however, to point out that evil in James is frequently a social rather than an individual force. His recognition of evil in institutionalized society, usually that of Europe, where in spite of its cultural and aesthetic graces, there is the "blackness of an old-world social order," [30] is usually reflected in fiction that reveals that appearances are deceptive: that manners are not morals and righteousness is not virtue. Whether James indicts the hypocrisy of French aristocracy, as he does in "Gabrielle de Bergerac" and *The American*, the degeneracy of such sophisticated milieux as those in *The Awkward Age* and "In the Cage," or the greed of such materialistic societies as those in *The Ivory Tower*, he reveals the disparity between the attractive exterior— the wealth, the manners, the social graces, and the evidences of culture—and the evil center. He repeatedly exposes what Maggie Verver calls "the thing hideously *behind*, behind so much trusted, so much pretended, nobleness, cleverness, tenderness" (XXIV, 237).

The sense of evil beneath the gilded surfaces of society is paralleled by the detection of evil in moral righteousness. Often this notion is portrayed comically, especially in such Puritanical Americans as Mr. Babcock, the itinerant New England minister in *The American,* and Waymarsh in *The Ambassadors,* but more often than not James points out the power for evil of the self-righteous. James treats this theme too by contrasting appearance and reality. In any number of stories he shows the ostensibly "good," those whose behavior is approved by society, to be in fact capable of the worst kind of evil. Thus the narrow-minded wife of Mark Ambient in "The Author of Beltraffio" sacrifices both husband and child in adherence to her warped notion of morality. Mrs. Newsome in *The Ambassadors* and Olive Chancellor of *The Bostonians* are additional illustrations of the tyranny of self-righteousness.

In all of James's fiction, if the villains are motivated by common and frequently vulgar desires, the human damage is irreparable. The victim suffers for more than loss of material possessions. He suffers loss of love, as does Newman, or loss of life, as does Isabel Archer spiritually and Milly Theale physically. Fleda Vetch's loss of the spoils of Poynton and of Owen Gereth causes not only solitude and poverty but intense spiritual suffering. The effect of evil is usually to cut off the victim from free experience and permanently ruin his chances for happiness.

Though James alters the traditional Puritan consideration of evil by focusing on the sinned-against rather than the sinner, he perhaps even more than Hawthorne reflects a Puritan view of life in the dominant pattern of his novels, his view of life as a kind of pilgrimage. We may well be reminded of Bunyan or the New England historians in following a James hero through his experience, in which he is called upon to exercise supreme moral discrimination on a road beset with evil. Like Milton, James rejected the notion of a "cloistered virtue" and sent his innocents into the world to prove themselves: not simply to resist temptation but to encounter experience, to face evil, to suffer, to endure, to exercise and retain the moral view of life, and by doing so ultimately to achieve salvation. Obviously the doctrinal ideas of the Puritan allegorists and historians are not present in James, but his view of life as the trial of the individual is essentially the same.

The notion of life as a trial is implicitly related to one of James's primary themes: the necessity of experience. The exhortation of

Strether to Bilham in *The Ambassadors*—"Live all you can; it's a mistake not to. It doesn't so much matter what you do in particular, so long as you have your life" (XXI, 217)—is neither a plea for hedonism nor for aestheticism, and certainly not a plea for personality development through a variety of secular experiences. Isabel Archer of *The Portrait of a Lady* explains the Jamesian principle of experience:

> "I'm not bent on a life of misery. . . . I've always been intensely determined to be happy, and I've often believed I should be. . . . But it comes over me every now and then that I can never be happy in any extraordinary way; not by turning away, by separating myself . . . from life, . . . from the usual chances and dangers, from what most people know and suffer" (III, 187).

To miss experience, as does John Marcher of "The Beast in the Jungle," "the man of his time, *the* man, to whom nothing on earth was to have happened" (XVIII, 125), is to stultify one's self, to make moral development impossible, to starve the consciousness, to become sterile and spiritually dead.

James's principle of experience represents a belief in the expansion of consciousness, for the subjective life of the individual, his reflections and recognitions, his emotional responses to experience, comprise the essential life of James's fiction. The maturing of the moral consciousness through experience enables James's heroes and heroines to triumph over evil spiritually though they are otherwise defeated by it. Proper moral growth can occur only with an encounter with evil. Though the exposure of the innocent to evil involves loss and suffering, the result—the expanded consciousness—represents an ultimate victory.

The suggestion that James's fiction has the recurrent theme of the "fortunate fall" leads almost inevitably to a reference to R. W. B. Lewis's *The American Adam*, which fully examines the uses of "the Adamic mythology" in American literature, and in a few pages relates James to the tradition. Professor Lewis writes, "The form which life assumed in James's fiction reflected the peculiarly American rhythm of the Adamic experience: the birth of the innocent, the foray into the unknown world, the collision with that world, 'the fortunate fall,' the wisdom and the maturity which suffering produced." [31] Self-development, however, regardless of how spiritual and moral that development may be, in no way negates the ugliness of the evil which helped bring it about. James's fiction represents, if not the synthesis, certainly the coexistence of a Puritan concern with evil and a transcendentalist concern with experience.

Evil in James's fiction acquires its intensity not by the mere documentation of facts, but by the means employed to make the facts significant. Throughout his career James employed a variety of fictional methods to intensify situations and to give them universal implications. He grew increasingly adept at utilizing imagery and symbolism and at suggesting mythical parallels to his plots in order to give his material the widest relevance.[32] He frequently relied on such primitive plot substructures as the fairy story, the fable, and the melodrama [33] in order to reveal that beneath the impeccable manners and sophisticated dialogue of his characters there lurked the most basic of conflicts, that between good and evil; and his many methods enabled him to dramatize that conflict in its elemental force.

James's principal means of intensifying evil, however, was to reveal its emotional effect on the character who is its victim. "Henry James mentalized phenomena," writes A. C. Orage.[34] When James converts the concrete fact of evil into a kind of impalpable essence, the effect is not to diminish its reality but to intensify it by making it mysterious—even vaguely supernatural. Even when the nature of a crime is specified, like the duplicity of the Bellegardes or the parasitism of Gilbert Osmond, the sense of the evil far transcends the recorded facts, for as the evil impresses itself on the consciousness of the victim, the reader is compelled to realize its full force through the emotional reaction of the sinned-against. Sometimes, as in "The Turn of the Screw," the precise nature of the offense is not told us. James explains in the preface to the tale that to describe "the offered example, the imputed vice, the cited act" is to make evil limited and credible; "Only make the reader's general vision of evil intense enough . . . and his own experience, his own imagination, his own sym-

pathy . . . and horror . . . will supply him quite sufficiently
with all the particulars. Make him *think* the evil, make him think
it for himself, and you are released from weak specifications." [35]
James accomplishes these ends in this tale by making full use of
the consciousness of the governess, whose terror colors her
response to the experience and passes it on in turn to the reader.

Subjective response to evil is not simply a means of gaining
intensity; it is related to James's notion that phenomena are only
important when the private consciousness contains them. In a
sense evil does not exist outside the mind of the spectator, who
may be either a victim or witness. Probably the most intense sense
of evil in James's fiction occurs at those times, which are frequent,
when we witness the individual sensibility reacting to evil. In such
scenes as that in which Isabel Archer sits before the fireplace and
reflects upon Osmond's deception of her, we see what L. C.
Knights terms James's "preoccupation with the plight of the
trapped creature," the person who can only passively suffer. It is
this "sense of suffocation" [36] that isolates the spectator from the
movement of life that testifies most fully to James's imaginative
grasp of the power of evil.

CHAPTER TWO

Evil and the International Theme

IT IS NOT difficult to explain Henry James's preoccupation with the international theme. As a historian of his times, James found considerably more meaning and interest than his contemporaries in the spectacles of international marriages and American tourists in Europe. Furthermore, James habitually saw human experience in terms of contraries. Through his repeated use of the international theme he gave cultural and national embodiment to the oppositions of innocence and experience, self and society, and good and evil which provide the dramatic tensions in all his works. The international theme offered James an inherent contrast between the most significant and extensive realities of his time.

"On the interest of *contrasted* things any painter of life and manners inevitably much depends, and contrast, fortunately for him, is easy to seek and to recognize," James writes; "the only difficulty is in presenting it again with effect, in extracting from it its sense and its lesson." [1] The "sense" and the "lesson" of the international theme are the moral issues involved in a conflict of representative national figures; for, while social comedy rules a story like "The Point of View," moral drama rules the more typical "A London Life." In most of his international fiction James penetrates the comic surface to the ethical conflict beneath. Thus such stories as "Daisy Miller," "The Reverberator," and "An International Episode," which expose American provincialism and offended European propriety, derive their "sense" and their "lesson" from James's profound concern with the nature of good and evil.

In the international fiction James identifies both good and evil with specific nations and cultures; more precisely, there are versions of good and evil peculiarly American, and versions peculiarly European. Though the Europeans are no matches for the Americans in ethical conduct, both have their generic malignities. Thus it is far from adequate to hold that James's America is good and his Europe evil, though it is generally true that the evil of Europe is more prominent than that of America. Actually James gains variety and subtlety in his international fiction through his concern with the many forms of evil he finds in American life, while there is a certain sameness and melodramatic obviousness in his treatment of the evil of Europe.

The basic pattern of James's international fiction is well known and requires only a brief description here. The American has an instinctive moral sense; yet he is offered no means for experience, no possibility of development. When he journeys to Europe, the American is exposed to a rich complexity of art, history, and manners, but also to an evil inseparable from the age and beauty which he has sought. The American responds either by renouncing Europe on account of its evil, or by renouncing the moral sense on account of Europe. The pursuit of happiness and experience leads to the crucial moral choice—the decision between the world and the self. No synthesis between American innocence and European experience is possible.

AMERICA: VERSIONS OF OPPRESSION

As complexity is the most obvious characteristic of James's Europe, simplicity is the most striking feature of his America. It is a simplicity which excludes not only all the social and cultural advantages catalogued in the well known passage in James's *Hawthorne*, but also the evil inherent in traditional society. In "An International Episode" (1879), two English visitors to Newport gain impressions of

> images of early breezy shining hours on lawns and piazzas
> that overlooked the sea; of innumerable pretty girls saying
> innumerable quaint and familiar things; of infinite lounging
> and talking and laughing and flirting and lunching and din-
> ing; of a confidence that broke down, of a freedom that

pulled up, nowhere; of an idyllic ease that was somehow too
ordered for a primitive social consciousness and too innocent
for a developed; of occasions on which they so knew every
one and every thing that they almost ached with reciprocity;
of drives and rides in the late afternoon, over gleaming
beaches, on long sea-roads, beneath a sky lighted up by
marvellous sunsets; of tea-tables, on the return, informal,
irregular, agreeable; of evenings at open windows or on the
perpetual verandahs, in the summer starlight, above the warm
Atlantic and amid irrelevant outbursts of clever minstrelsy.
. . . it was all the book of life, of American life, at least; with
the chapter of "complications" bodily omitted (XIV, 320).

The simple beauty of the idyllic pastoral scene is consistent with,
if not symbolic of, the innocence of its inhabitants. At its best
James's America is a kind of Eden, in which refinement, intelligence, and morality are natural endowments, uninhibited by any
external social or religious code. This to James is the perfectly
organic society, for there can be no distinction between man as
social creature and man as individual. Society derives its character from the individuals comprising it; no system of manners and
morals shapes the members or limits them.

In *A Small Boy and Others* (1913), in which James recollects
the charm of the America of his youth, he speaks of his cousin
Helen as a representative of this uncomplicated society: "I note
with appreciation that she was strenuously, actively good, and
have the liveliest impression both that no one was ever better, and
that her goodness somehow testifies for the whole tone of a society, a remarkable cluster of private decencies." Some pages
later James writes, "The social scheme, as we knew it, was, in its
careless charity, worthy of the golden age . . . ." The merit of
this ideal American society is that its principles of conduct are
private rather than public, spontaneous rather than cultivated,
simple rather than complex; in the narrow sense of the word it is
no society at all, rather a kind of anarchy: "How as mere detached unaccompanied infants we enjoyed such impunity of
range and confidence of welcome is beyond comprehension save
by the light of the old [American] manners and conditions, the

old local bonhomie, the comparatively primal innocence, the absence of complications . . . ."[2]

The America of "An International Episode" and *Notes of a Son and Brother*, as well as other of James's works, is the idealized myth, the America of the romancer, concerned with spiritual rather than surface truth; and, as R. W. B. Lewis has made clear, the mythology is Adamic.[3] The central reality beneath the romantic surface is the innocence of the American, an innocence nurtured and guarded by the very lack of "a complex social machinery"[4] that James found necessary for the artist. But if freedom and innocence are negative virtues, they are inestimable ones and abound in "a little world of easy and happy interchange, of unrestricted and yet all so instinctively sane and secure association and conversation, with all its liberties and delicacies, all its mirth and earnestness protected and directed so much more from within than from without . . . ."[5]

The conflict, or dialectic, of the international theme involves the collision of the internal code with the external. In "An International Episode," for example, the American, Bessie Alden, is snubbed by the mother of the British nobleman who has proposed to her. Bessie's inherent sense of honor leads her to reject the proposal: British pride in name and station clashes with American pride in self.

Aside from the simple and innocent America of the Adamic myth, there is also the America of oppression and evil in James's work. In the main, James finds evil, like good, to be a product of freedom: it is an effect of self-coercion rather than external pressure. It is the moral sense gone wrong and innocence perverted; it comes from a consideration of American negations as fulfillments and inflexible codes. In extreme, the evil of America is an intense provincialism that breeds aggressive narrow-mindedness; in moderation it is a complacent ignorance of the value of foreign experience.

The New England conscience, even though James frequently exposes it comically, is a source of evil in his fiction. Through Benjamin Babcock of *The American* (1877) James parodies the excessive moral timidity of the overdeveloped con-

science, but even in the case of Babcock there is evidence of an
evil, for though his shortsightedness is foolish to Christopher
Newman, it is oppressive to Babcock, who is attracted to art by
his aesthetic sensibilities and pulled away from it by his inclination to suspect all pleasure and beauty.

In *The Europeans* (1878), the Puritan temperament is for the
most part either absurd or quaint. A characteristic touch is the
conversation between Mr. Wentworth, with his inherited distrust
of art and leisure, and the European Felix Young, who requests
that he be allowed to paint the old man's portrait:

> "I think sitting for one's portrait is only one of the various
> forms of idleness," said Mr. Wentworth. "Their name is
> legion."
> "My dear sir," cried Felix, "you can't be said to idle when
> you are making a man work so!"
> "One might be painted while one is asleep," suggested Mr.
> Brand, as a contribution to the discussion.[6]

The Wentworth household is ruled by a fixed idea. Here is a case
in which innocence does not imply freedom; the family's hostility to free experience makes moral maturity impossible. There is
only physical freedom among the Wentworths, no intellectual
freedom. A number of death images suggest the real condition of
the family: Felix tells his sister, "My uncle, Mr. Wentworth . . .
looks as if he were undergoing martyrdom, not by fire, but by
freezing"; later Felix "perceived that there was something almost
cadaverous in his uncle's high-featured white face"; to the Baroness, Felix's sister, "Gertrude seemed . . . most funereal . . . ."[7]

The Wentworths' rigid morality, which just falls short of being
intolerance, expresses their fear of experience. Since life is tainted
by evil, the Wentworths choose not to live at all; they shelter
themselves from their European guests, who in turn invite them
to share in the happiness and fullness of their lives. Felix Young
is the normative character, opposed on the one hand by his sister,
an adventuress who is not above deception, and on the other by
the Wentworths, who equate happiness with evil. Felix admires
the freshness but regrets the gloominess of the Americans. He
tells Gertrude,

"You seem to me very well placed, for enjoying. You have money and liberty and what is called in Europe a 'position.' But you take a painful view of life, as you may say."

"One ought to think it bright and charming and delightful, eh?" asked Gertrude.

"I should say so—if one can. It is true it all depends on that," Felix added.

"You know there is a great deal of misery in the world," said his model.

"I have seen a little of it," the young man rejoined. "But it was all over there—beyond the sea. I don't see any here. This is a paradise.". . .

"To 'enjoy,'" [Gertrude said,] "to take life—not painfully, must one do something wrong?"

Felix gave his long light laugh again. "Seriously, I think not. And for this reason, among others: you strike me as very capable of enjoying, if the chances were given you, and yet at the same time as incapable of wrong-doing." [8]

Gertrude then, according to Felix, should view life as an opportunity rather than a discipline.

Among the Americans in *The Europeans,* only Gertrude breaks away from the stiff moral environment to seek a fuller experience; she marries Felix and goes with him to Europe, where conceivably her innate virtue and intelligence will be allowed to mature. Mr. Wentworth is beyond salvation; he is, as Felix observes, spiritually dead. Charlotte, Gertrude's sister, and Mr. Brand, the clergyman who unsuccessfully courted Gertrude, are alike unchanged by the Europeans and remain incapable of moral growth. Robert Acton, a neighbor of the Wentworths but apparently far more liberal and sophisticated than they, is equally subdued by his conscience. He falls in love with the Baroness Münster and thinks of marrying her. The Baroness, whose motive in visiting her relatives is to gain a fortune, would welcome the marriage, for Acton is very wealthy. Acton rejects the Baroness when he discovers that she is capable of lying; but the Baroness's lies are harmless, usually motivated by good manners.[9] As Rebecca West points out, "poor Eugenia fails altogether in an environment where a lie from her lips is not treated as *un petit péché d'une petite femme*, but remains simply a lie." [10] Acton is really worse than the Wentworths in that he is compelled by conscience to chastise others as well as shelter himself.

In Acton's repudiation of the Baroness, the inflexible virtue of the New Englander has become perverted and destructive; negative virtue has become active evil. For the most part the New England conscience is evil only to the extent that it prohibits experience. But it cannot be assumed that such an abstract basis of morality as the Wentworths' remains simply quaint when transferred to foreign soil or when influenced by alien codes. Thus Gertrude shows that she has no adequate substitute for the discipline she has abandoned. The New England morality is the only morality she knows; she has no personal resources to fall back upon. James clearly shows that the marriage of Gertrude and Felix is far from an ideal union of American innocence and European experience, for Gertrude from the start uses her newly found freedom to injure the representatives of her old code. She crudely insults Mr. Brand and Charlotte, and is brash and inconsiderate to everyone. It is not simply that Gertrude knows nothing of delicacy or tact, but that she is unable to reconcile her old standards of moral decency with the exuberant experience that Felix makes attainable.

The Europeans ends when Gertrude marries, and we are not told what she experiences in Europe. But in "A London Life" (1888), there is an American woman very much like Gertrude whose response to her European experience reveals the grave limitations in American innocence. Laura Wing, a young sheltered American with a New England conscience, visits her sister in London, where she finds herself in the midst of a thoroughly scandalous situation: her sister and her brother-in-law are both openly engaged in adultery. Laura is shocked and on the point of collapse. But her conduct surpasses indignation: to keep herself above any suspicion of impropriety she hysterically exhorts her relatives to reform and crudely tries to persuade a young American to marry her. James's opinion of his heroine is necessarily ambiguous, however, for as the center of consciousness in the story the righteous Laura is not inclined to question her own

conduct. There is only one occasion when Laura considers that
her interference might be reprehensible:

> Was she all wrong after all—was she cruel by being too
> rigid? . . . ought she only to propose to herself to "al-
> low" more and more, and to allow ever, and to smooth things
> down by gentleness, by sympathy, by not looking at them
> too hard? It was not the first time the just measure seemed
> to slip from her hands as she became conscious of possible,
> or rather of very actual, differences of standard and usage
> (X, 372).

Laura, however, chooses intervention over endurance. Though
her reckless attempts at reform are explicable in terms of her
emotionally starved and morally rigorous past, Laura has something in common with the sophisticated evildoers of *The American* and *The Portrait of a Lady*: that is, she will not be content
until she imposes her own narrow standards on others. It is nearly
an inflexible rule in James's fiction that regardless of one's intentions he must respect the freedom of others. Through her meddling, Laura brings shame and hostility only to herself, yet she
demonstrates the potential power for evil in the innocent who
takes it upon himself to generalize from his own creed and to
judge and reform others.

The New England ethos is more specifically under attack in
The Bostonians (1886). Olive Chancellor's devotion to the abstract cause of woman's rights leads her to frustrate the impres-
sionable Verena Tarrant's impulses to love. Oppression is clearly
the dominant mood of *The Bostonians*. As opposed to the fresh
and open scene of *The Europeans*, the settings in *The Bostonians*
are for the most part musty and enclosed. In Olive's parlor the
hero, Basil Ransom, thinks he has "never seen an interior that was
so much an interior as this queer corridor-shaped drawing room
of his new-found kinswoman . . . ." Most of the story takes
place in such rooms, or in narrow, low-ceilinged lecture halls,
where the audience has "an anxious, haggard look, though there
were sundry exceptions—half a dozen placid, florid faces." Boston itself is cold, decayed, and drab:

The western windows of Olive's drawing room, looking over the water, took in the red sunsets of winter; the long, low bridge that crawled, on its staggering posts, across the Charles; the casual patches of ice and snow; the desolate suburban horizons, peeled and made bald by the rigour of the season; the general hard, cold void of the prospect; the extrusion, at Charlestown, at Cambridge, of a few chimneys and steeples, straight, sordid tubes of factories and engine-shops, or spare, heavenward finger of the New England meeting house. There was something inexorable in the poverty of the scene, shameful in the meanness of its details, which gave a collective impression of boards and tin and frozen earth, sheds and rotting piles, railwaylines striding flat across a thoroughfare of puddles, and tracks of the humbler, the universal horse-car, traversing obliquely this path of danger; loose fences, vacant lots, mounds of refuse, yards bestrewn with iron pipes, telegraph poles, and bare wooden backs of places.[11]

Ransom attempts to liberate Verena from Olive and from Boston. Symbolically his meetings with her occur in parks or on the Harvard campus, where Verena can not only breathe fresh air, but also enjoy a freedom from the movement which supports her liberty. The central situation of Olive's repression of Verena, not to mention her far more perverse self-repression, fuses with the New England urban setting to reveal the moral decay of Boston in a way that looks forward to poetic treatments of the same theme by T. S. Eliot and Robert Lowell.

In his remark that "the society of Boston was and is quite uncivilized but refined beyond the point of civilization," T. S. Eliot [12] refers to the New England tendency to dissociate morality from experience, the same habit of mind which James exposes in *The Europeans*. In *The Bostonians* he exposes a later generation of New Englanders, involved in post-Civil War urbanization and commercialism, rabidly progressive rather than primly conservative. The Calvinistic zeal has found political and secular expression. But, to return to Eliot's observation, the moral and social barbarism of the Boston James depicts is but the outgrowth of the refinement of a slightly earlier stage of New England culture. In neither era has the New England conscience adapted itself to the demands of personal liberty and social experience.

The world represented by Verena Tarrant's parents is the world of money. In their gross commercialism, Selah Tarrant, a fake mesmerist who exploits his daughter's public-speaking ability, and his wife, a tawdry social climber who hopes to crash society through Olive's adoption (actually purchase) of her daughter, reveal the ultimate corruption of New England Puritanism. The Tarrants seem remote from both the serene dignity of the Wentworths and the misguided idealism of Olive. If Mr. Wentworth and Olive represent a society which has abstracted ethics from experience and morals from manners, the Tarrants represent a society supported by neither ethics nor manners. They repel morally and aesthetically. They are the end product of a people who have never been able to reconcile the demands of the world with those of religion.

When morals go wrong in New England, and to some degree in America as a whole, James implies, the result is an intolerable vulgarity as well as a destructive evil. For the most part James's European malefactors pay great heed to manners, to a civilized style; indeed they repeatedly sacrifice conscience to form. But New England has a long tradition of hostility to beauty, and thus when it changes from a leisurely to an acquisitive society it can only be vulgar. In good and evil alike, the New Englander has no concern for appearances; they always correspond with reality.

The Tarrants, therefore, are an implicit criticism of the New England mind. But more specifically they cast a shadow on the liberalism of Miss Birdseye, Olive, and their fellow enthusiasts. The Tarrants are knaves and the others fools, but both feminism and mesmerism oppress the innocent, Verena, and both are condemned by the wise witness, Ransom.

The Tarrants are perhaps the most appalling examples of vulgarity in James's fiction, mainly because their lack of any aesthetic sense is all but identical with their lack of any moral sense. This, however, is using the term "vulgarity" in a simpler way than James himself uses it. "Vulgarity," in his fiction, is a term of

both moral and aesthetic disapprobation. James frequently describes moral or immoral conduct in aesthetic terminology:
"ugly" is almost synonymous with "evil," and "beautiful" with
"good." This practice, however, should not be interpreted to
mean that James considers vulgarity per se evil, and refinement
per se good. It is incorrect to assume with H. R. Hays that "James
really felt that bad manners was worse than murder," [13] or with
Ernest A. Baker that in James's fiction "Vulgarity is the flesh and
the devil." [14] James is in the tradition not of Oscar Wilde ("It is
absurd to divide people into good and bad. People are either
charming or tedious" [15] but in the tradition of Emerson ("Beauty
is the mark God sets upon virtue" [16]).

In James's fiction vulgarity is mainly an American trait. At
times it accompanies provincialism, as with the unsophisticated
and self-satisfied Marcellus Cockeral of "The Point of View"
(1882), who complacently rejects all of Europe: "They talk
about things that we've settled ages ago, and the solemnity with
which they propound to you their little embarrassments makes a
heavy draft on one's good nature" (XIV, 599). At other times
vulgarity indicates moral barbarism. Just as the bad manners of
Verena Tarrant's parents reflect their greed, fraudulence, and indecency, so George Flack, an American correspondent for the
scandal sheet *The Reverberator*, in the story of the same name
(1888), has a brashness and indelicacy which mirror his moral
corruption. As a journalist—one of many in James, all of whom
(except Merton Densher) commit the arch crime of invading
privacy—he delights in betraying confidences and exposing
secrets. It is difficult to point out where Flack's vulgarity—his
passion for money, scandal, and publicity—ends and where his
immorality—his violation of privacy—begins; he is vulgar because he is immoral and immoral because he is vulgar.

Frequently vulgarity is accompanied by acquisitiveness: not
the desire for experience, for the sense of the past, or for happiness which incites so many of James's American heroines on their
European pilgrimages, but simply a greed for things. The wife
and daughter of Mr. Ruck, the American business man in "The
Pension Beaurepas" (1879), are devastating caricatures of a century of American woman tourists in Europe, armed with cameras

and checkbooks, and blind to all but size and quantity. James's treatment, however, goes beyond caricature, for he reveals in the Ruck women a vicious selfishness and an unquenchable avarice that horrify rather than amuse. Mrs. Ruck and her daughter wish simply to buy Europe—to get as many of its clothes and jewels as possible. James dramatizes the sordid as well as the preposterous nature of this undertaking by showing the effect of the lavish spending on the pitiable husband. As one of the characters in the story says,

> To get something in a 'store' that they can put on their backs—that's their one idea; they haven't another in their heads. Of course they spend no end of money, and they do it with an implacable persistence, with a mixture of audacity and of cunning. They do it in his teeth and they do it behind his back; the mother protects the daughter, while the daughter eggs on the mother. Between them they're bleeding him to death (XIV, 460).

Vulgarity and immorality both stem from the same source, a fundamental blindness to all but the grossest of values. The Ruck women's tastelessness is but the converse of their disrespect for Mr. Ruck. Virtue always stands in some relation to awareness in James. In some cases aesthetic awareness may exist without moral awareness (for example, in Gilbert Osmond and Mrs. Gereth); in other cases a commonplace moral awareness may exist without aesthetic awareness (for example, in Henrietta Stackpole and Owen Gereth); but James's superior creatures combine the two (for example, Isabel Archer and Fleda Vetch). If the highest morality requires the unified sensibility, the basest immorality often results from some kind of imbalance between the aesthetic and the moral understanding, or from a deficiency in both.

The inoffensive vulgarians in James, those with a kind of moral sense, are agents of a mild evil. They oppress themselves. For good is necessarily imperfect in James unless it masters experience; and the vulgar by definition are incapable of experience. They see life superficially and they cannot participate in the refining and maturing process which the complex civilization offers. "Daisy Miller" (1878) is a story in which an apparently inoffensive, even charming, vulgarity is a moral limitation. Most commentators have stressed the victory of American innocence over narrow European standards. But Daisy does not profit from her experience; she is a pure child of nature, whose response to trivial and grave challenges alike is impulsive. Without conscious reflection Daisy disregards the dicta of the American colony in Rome that she should not appear in public with a gentleman unescorted, that she should not violate curfews, that she should not treat her courier as an equal. Daisy "does what she likes" because there is no other motivation in her simple nature. Innocent and good as she is, she has no moral, not to mention aesthetic, consciousness. She has neither receptivity nor potency. Her European travels, her relation to Winterbourne and to the offended Americans, and her indifference to convention are ultimately meaningless to her. She is a person on whom everything is lost.

3)   The business man in James has the same basic deficiency. Though James confessed that his inadequate knowledge of "the huge organized mystery of the consummately, the supremely applied money-passion" precluded his treating "nineteen-twentieths" [17] of American city life, another reason is probably James's belief that for the business man the "money-passion" is the only passion, that his business denies him the physical and intellectual freedom necessary for the enriching experience of Europe. Daisy Miller's father remains in Schenectady making money; Mr. Dosson of "The Reverberator," when not sitting idly in his hotel room, likes Europe because he can spend part of his fortune there: "he was never content on any occasion unless a great deal of money was spent . . ." (XIII, 50). Business is not a base activity to James until such late works as "The Jolly Corner" and *The Ivory Tower,* but in his early fiction it consistently stifles the spirit and the sensibilities. Ferner Nuhn, among other critics, has commented on James's "curious attitude toward money, which made the possession of worldly means—and a comfortable amount of it!—virtually a prerequisite for the good life, but the acquisition of it an almost necessarily damning activity." [18] The possession of money is a condition of freedom, and the earning of

✳ it a condition of slavery.

Thus money-making, like the New England conscience and provincial vulgarity, causes or reflects the deadened consciousness. An apt illustration is Mr. Ruck of "The Pension Beaurepas," described by a fellow tourist as "a broken-down man of business. He's broken-down in health and I think he must be broken-down in fortune. He has spent his whole life in buying and selling and watching prices, so that he knows how to do nothing else" (XIV, 460). There is some comedy in Mr. Ruck's pathetic incompatibility with the leisurely and cultured life in Europe: "Well, we certainly saw the cathedral. I don't know as we're any the better for it, and I don't know as I should know it again. But we saw it anyway, stone by stone—and heard about it century by century" (XIV, 440). But there is minor tragedy in the old man's approaching bankruptcy as his wife and daughter spend the last of his dollars on clothes and jewelry which they will never use. Mr. Ruck is figuratively and literally killed by money, by the possession of it and by the lack of it.

In James's early work the wealthy business man is usually seen as an innocent soul spiritually blighted by his work. The unsuccessful business man, however, is most often a conniver and a scoundrel. George Fenton of *Watch and Ward* (1878) and Morris Townsend of *Washington Square* (1880), both failures in business, try to marry for money. When James returned to the American scene in his later years his critical insight into the nature of business deepened, so that he went beyond the rather limited— and unmistakably middle-class—attitude of regarding business success as a certain key to morality and business failure as a clear indication of immorality.

Fenton and Townsend are exceptions, however, to the general rule that evil in American life comes from prohibition and restraint, rather than aggression and intervention. Thus commercialism is usually a negative rather than a positive evil: it is hostile to experience and moral development. All of James's Americans who commit themselves to a specific code or cause—whether it be New England Puritanism, feminism, commercialism, or nationalism—are incompletely human. And in this respect James shares the belief of his philosopher-theologian father, who, as his novelist son was to write, insisted that "What we were to do . . .

was just to be something, something unconnected with specific doing, something free and uncommitted, something finer in short than *being that*, whatever it was, might consist of." [19] Those who choose to be something specific are unable to be themselves; by adhering to an external system they unfit themselves to live the inner life.

James's fictional portraits of America and Americans give abundant support to the observation of M. D. Zabel that "The American mind, rooted in hereditary conscience, had never escaped its hauntings by darker powers, its stirring of ancestral guilt, what Howells was presently to call 'the slavery implicated in our liberty.' " [20] Some of James's stories imply the existence of an evil inherent in American life beyond individual control and considerably less tangible than the various evils of commerce, vulgarity, and Puritanism, although it is perhaps the ultimate source of them. In remembering his American youth, James reflects on "the relics of those we have seen beaten," on "the chronicle of early deaths, arrested careers, broken promises, orphaned children," and on those who "in spite of brilliant promise and romantic charm, ended badly, as badly as possible." [21] Pertinently, Van Wyck Brooks writes, "To the end of his life . . . America, to James, signified destruction and failure. It was the dark country, where the earth was a quicksand, where amiable uncles ended in disaster, where men were turned into machines, where genius was subject to all sorts of inscrutable catastrophes." [22] James interpreted the failures and disasters of his friends and relatives as somehow symbolic of an intrinsic treachery in America. [23]

Thus the evil of America in "A Passionate Pilgrim," "Europe," "Four Meetings," and *Washington Square* cannot be explained as the effect of self-suppression; the protagonists of these stories are suppressed by various external, rather than internal, agencies. In his discussion of *The Portrait of a Lady*, Pelham Edgar complains (rather unreasonably) that

> There is not much to be gained by portraying a woman with a mind, if that mind is ultimately to be cramped in its opportunity for growth, nor in emphasizing the value of

experience, if experience is to lead in the end to a spiritual prison in which the natural impulses of the heart must suffer an inevitable decay.[24]

According to his own standards, Edgar should find even more intolerable those James stories in which persons of sensibility and intelligence must accept spiritual imprisonment from the start. Such characters are never allowed to reach the point where they can choose to renounce or accept happiness; they are thwarted, not by free will, but by something like fate.

One example is Clement Searle, the decayed, brittle, and sensitive hero of "A Passionate Pilgrim" (1871) who is deprived of his hereditary right to an English manor by a proud cousin who schemes to keep the estate in his own hands. Because he is poor, Searle is unable to leave America. His bad health symbolizes the effect of American life on his spirit. When Searle finally comes to England, believing he can recover his estate, the incivility of the British relative is all that is needed to kill both body and spirit. Searle, then, who requires a richness of culture and manners to sustain his fine consciousness, is to a large degree destroyed by the aesthetic poverty of America.

"Four Meetings" (1877) and "Europe" (1899) are slight and ironic stories of frustration; each deals with a young woman of imagination and intelligence who is prevented—in "Four Meetings" by inadequate finances and in "Europe" by family obligations—from going to Europe, an experience which, James implies, is necessary for the spiritual and intellectual growth of each. The irony in these stories is that the generosity of these two women keeps them from fulfilling their ambitions. Jane Rimmle, who has an intense "sense of life" (XVI, 354), wastes away in New England caring for her mother, who is constantly ill but never dies; Caroline Spencer, a New England schoolteacher, uses her life savings to take a trip to Europe, but she gets only as far as Le Havre, where she gives her money to her worthless cousin so that he may pay his debts.

Catherine Sloper of *Washington Square* (1880) is James's most fully realized portrait of the person frustrated by external forces. Catherine is coerced by her father, who if not a tyrant is a cold-

blooded analyst who trades upon the respect Catherine has for
him, by Miss Penniman, her witless and meddlesome aunt, and by
Morris Townsend, the adventurer who wants to marry the unattractive Catherine for her money. Catherine is betrayed by her
innocence and unawareness and by the essentially well inten-
tioned interference of her father and aunt as much as she is by the
deceit of Townsend. Unlike most of James's heroines, Catherine
is not allowed the freedom to make a mistake. Though her father's judgment is correct, we feel that he creates for Catherine a
harsher and sadder life than she would have had with Townsend.
If she is sheltered from disillusion, she is also sheltered from the
moral experience of making a decision and living with it.

Like Caroline Spencer and Jane Rimmle, Catherine misses "living" partly because she is good; she is incapable of disobeying her
father. While in *The Portrait of a Lady* the native moral sense
prevents an unqualified acceptance of "the ampler experience" [25]
of Europe, in *Washington Square* it prevents the slightest movement toward experience. Unlike the Wentworths, Catherine is
restrained, not by a New England conscience, but by a clear-
headed concept of loyalty. Were Catherine to disobey her father,
she would certainly lose our sympathy. Nor should we think that
a deficiency in intellect is the major impediment to Catherine's
development; rather it is a deficiency in freedom.

In the end Catherine accepts her fate, her life-in-death. Her
experience has been one solely of suffering and frustration:

> From her own point of view the great facts of her career were
> that Morris Townsend had trifled with her affection, and
> that her father had broken its spring. Nothing could ever
> alter these facts; they were always there, like her name, her
> age, her plain face. Nothing could ever undo the wrong or
> cure the pain that Morris had inflicted on her, and nothing
> could ever make her feel toward her father as she felt in her
> younger years. There was something dead in her life, and her
> duty was to try and fill the void.[26]

Catherine can rise above self-pity, but not above suffering, the
permanent scar of evil. But her suffering is almost entirely gratuitous, the effect of environment rather than free choice. Catherine

acquires a kind of moral strength and stoic wisdom through her sad history, but her life is primarily one of wasted sensibilities.

In the main, however, the American protagonist has the freedom to realize his ideals. But just as the evil which can oppress the American is most often a negation, so too the free American possesses a good which is negative: [27] he is blissfully ignorant of evil; he is uninfluenced by weighty codes of manners and ethics. The ideal American is capable of "living," of responding to the splendor of Europe, and of enriching his moral-aesthetic consciousness through the experience it offers.

Among the Americans who have the freedom and the intelligence to seek the prizes of Europe there are different character types and modes of behavior. There are those who either respond too much to Europe or not enough, and those who maintain the delicate balance between conscience and experience. Implicit in the international theme is the tension between what Elizabeth Stevenson calls

> the conscious individual and the raw material of life. That person has two duties in living: the first, to expose himself to as much of the great unconscious force of life as he is able to endure; the second, to hold firm to that irreducible core which is himself, to be what he is with all his might.[28]

Most of the Americans who are cramped by a literal and dogmatic morality stay in America; but if they go to Europe, their major concern is to protect themselves from any personal involvement. They remain uncommitted and untested. Rowland Mallet, for example, can gain experience only vicariously, through his protégé Roderick Hudson. He enjoys the art and culture of Europe, but shies away from any human relationship, so that in the end his fear of life has prevented him from marrying.

At the opposite pole is Winterbourne of "Daisy Miller." Like Mallet he is restrained from marriage by a perversion of scruples, but his suspicion and aversion are caused not by an exaggeration but by a withering of the American moral sense. He is an American who, in repudiating Daisy Miller, commits the arch European crime of judging on appearances. If Mallet, and also Robert Acton

of *The Europeans,* remain unmarried for having been too long in
New England, Winterbourne's fault is that he has lived too long
in Europe.

But the American can be too indiscriminate. Thus it is that the
Europeanized American is more often the agent of evil than the
European in James. There are the Americans who, far from remaining passive and suspicious, are unrestrained in their greed for
the riches of Europe. In *Roderick Hudson* (1875) both Mrs.
Light and her daughter Christina so totally adopt European
values that they deny American values. Mrs. Light coerces her
daughter into a profitable marriage to an Italian nobleman; Christina is so reckless and conscienceless in her craving for sensations
that she ruins Roderick Hudson and—in *The Princess Casamassima*—Hyacinth Robinson.

The American abroad exposes himself to the alternate possibilities of being betrayed by Europe and of losing his native integrity. He can become either victim or agent of evil. The European
is more restrained in his treachery, for the American retains his
freedom when he loses the rectitude usually coordinate with it.
The European must at least respect his own conventions, and his
aesthetic sense prohibits overt grossness. The Bellegardes' code of
honor may seem narrow and amoral; but the Osmonds and Lights
have no traditional codes.

Furthermore, James seems more interested in America than in
Europe in his international works. He reveals the many forms the
American character can assume when exposed to the complexity
of Europe. On the other hand, his Europeans are by contrast both
less interesting and less important; they form a kind of uniform
background to the multifaceted American temperament.

THE AMBIGUITY OF EUROPE

The foremost European sin is exclusiveness. The reprehensible
Europeans derive their standards externally, and betray and exploit in order to uphold them. Both the merits and the faults of
Europe are social rather than private. Europe represents culture,
civilization, art, and manners. One cannot make a simple distinction—as do James's more parochial Americans—between the
form and the content of Europe, and conclude that the form is

superficial because it masks the evil beneath. In James's
the exterior beauty always permits and frequently depend
treachery. Yet the surface has a reality of its own. European culture can be defined only as an ambiguity: it elevates normal human intercourse and social existence to a relation with beauty and
style, and yet private moral conduct inevitably undergoes a deg-
radation in order for the relation to be maintained. Ultimately
James finds perversion in the sacrifice of morals to manners, but
he never questions the importance of manners. His international
fiction explores the dilemma but never resolves it; the dialectical
opposition of American innocence and European experience is
unresolvable. In Ferner Nuhn's terms, "Europe is form without
spirit, America is spirit without form"; [29] and those who deny the
importance of form are as wrong as those who deny the importance of spirit. James's international fiction implies the failure of
western civilization, for its most searching implication is the dis-
cord between individual and society. The self-determined individual must deny the wellsprings of his being to partake of the
civilized society; those who refuse to make the compromise—the
Isabel Archers and Christopher Newmans—have no alternative
other than social and spiritual isolation.

The American's experience with Europe is one of disillusion,
for each must make his own discovery of the disparity between
appearance and reality. Laura Wing's recognition is typical:

> The contrast was before her again, the sense of the same curi-
> ous duplicity (in the literal meaning of the word) that she
> took in at Plash—the way the genius of such an old house was
> all peace and decorum and yet the spirit that prevailed there,
> outside the schoolroom, contentious and impure. She had
> often before been struck with this—with that perfection of
> machinery that can still at perfect times make English life go
> on of itself with a stately rhythm long after corruption is
> within it (X, 292).

The innocents themselves err in holding an impossible ideal—
their faults as well as their merits are idealistic. Clement Searle
assumes that the majestic exterior of an English country house
represents an ultimate kind of happiness; Euphemia Cleve is de-

luded by her romantic temperament into taking the faultless appearance and manners of the aristocrat Richard de Mauves at face value. Even before he meets European evil, the American is, in a sense, victimized by his own innocence.

The sense of evil is both more extreme and more apparent in Europe than in America. Employing—no doubt excessively—the melodramatic techniques of Dickens and Hawthorne, James suggests evil through scene rather than action. The once glittering aristocracy is now, quite literally, dark and crumbling. The spaciousness of the American's background contrasts with the narrowness of the European scene, just as American emotional spontaneity contrasts with European formality.

In "Madame de Mauves" (1874), for example, James develops meaning through scene; he depicts rather than dramatizes an evil considerably more extreme than the transgressions of Richard de Mauves—his marrying for money and his infidelity. James gains a certain depth and scope by suggesting that the heroine, symbolically named Euphemia, is coming into contact not with an isolated European but with the essence of European culture, so that the evil she experiences is one endemic to a civilization. Much of the story occurs in twilight, the time of day that is both night and day, or evil and good—suggesting the complexity of a society which offers external advantages if one is willing to accept the basic evil. The betrayed heroine consistently "linger[s] through the thickening twilight" (XIII, 220), inextricably trapped in the dense moral atmosphere. Originally Euphemia had been attracted to de Mauves because of the age of his family and home; it is, however, the evil of the past, decayed and corrupt, which injures her. The old formal garden is a kind of prison for her:

> She lived in an old-fashioned pavilion, between a high-walled court and an excessively artificial garden, between whose enclosure you saw a long line of tree-tops. . . . Presently she would come out and wander through the narrow alleys and beside the thin spouting fountain, and at last introduce [Longmore] to a private gate in a high wall, the opening to a gate which led to a forest (XIII, 244).

The forest means the same to Euphemia as Washington Square means to Catherine Sloper and the Harvard campus to Verena Tarrant: specifically it means freedom. But the forest is permanently closed to Euphemia, who must live out her life in the death scene, the walled-in formal garden with the ancient pavilion. She refuses to compromise her integrity to the code of the French family. In her white dress, she is the center of a picture: "her intrinsic clearness shone out . . . through the darker cast over it" (XIII, 251). The imagery throughout the story is conventional and its effectiveness is dubious, but James's effort to suggest that evil is inseparable from the European past is unmistakable.

It is noteworthy that whereas James frequently uses imagery of coldness, darkness, and imprisonment to symbolize the mysterious and pervasive evil of Europe, he is less concerned with scenic effects in those stories in which the Americans avoid injury by the Europeans. In "An International Episode," for instance, the situation is similar to that in *The American,* but the treatment is entirely different. The snobbish Duchess of Bayswater tries to prevent the marriage of her son to the American Bessie Alden. But since the Duchess is sketched in light rather than dark colors, her mistreatment of Bessie seems closer to bad taste than to evil; there is nothing to suggest a malignity more extreme than the overt—therefore limited—unpleasantness of the Duchess. The American can avoid suffering only from the less menacing forms of European culture. When he gets the better of the Europeans—notably in "An International Episode," "The Siege of London," "The Reverberator," and "Miss Gunton of Poughkeepsie"—he touches the surface of Europe, not the depths beneath.

The American

In *The American* (1877) James fully utilizes the inherent comic situation of the swaggering Californian in Europe: his ignorance of art and manners, his excessive good nature and optimism contrast sharply with his new environment. Christopher Newman is not only conventional and characteristic in his touring methods—in making Paris his headquarters and visiting the Louvre and the opera; he is also typically American in his attitude

toward Europe—in being candid and unashamed of his nationality, in desiring to "get something out of Europe," and in being
confident that he can conquer the world even though he knows
nothing about it. There is comedy and tragedy in James's drama
of the American abroad, but the common denominator or principle of unity is Newman's moral naïveté, his childlike ignorance
of the ways of the world. His gauche reactions to paintings and
cathedrals and the protocol of Parisian society are for the most
part highly comic; but his insensibility to European evil brings
about the moral struggle.

In the beginning Newman harbors the illusion that the world
is good, and evil nonexistent; he also assumes that he is a completely free agent, whose sole responsibility is to be as happy as
he possibly can. "The world [is] a great bazaar where one might
stroll about and purchase handsome things" (II, 87), Newman
believes. When he meets evil and suffers from it, Newman acquires a moral education; he is made to see the folly of his innocent illusions. One of the points of the novel is that, as in *Oedipus
Rex*, an ignorance of evil is a moral failure. It is the same message
Melville dramatizes in "Benito Cereno," in which the morally
immature Captain Delano is unable to recognize and understand
the evil inherent in the situation in which he is involved.

Newman wishes to take the best of Europe without dealing
with the worst of it. In Europe he wants "the biggest kind of en-
tertainment a man can get" (II, 33), and also

> "a great woman. I stick to that. That's one thing I *can*
> treat myself to, and if it's to be had I mean to have it. What
> else have I toiled and struggled for all these years? I've suc-
> ceeded, and now what am I to do with my success? To make
> it perfect, as I see it, there must be a lovely being perched on
> the pile like some shining statue crowning some high monu-
> ment. She must be as good as she's beautiful and as clever as
> she's good. I can give my wife many things, so I'm not afraid
> to ask certain others. . . . I want, in a word, the best article
> in the market" (II, 49).

The business metaphor is not accidental; it points to Newman's
basic fault, his tendency to deal with Europe and Europeans, if

not with life, as commodities for which he has the money to pay. Newman's good nature and boyish concern with fair play do not disguise his vanity. His self-satisfaction is finally identical with his innocence, for he cannot see that life ultimately demands more self-denial than that which the honest business man brings to bear in his purchases and sales.

In the beginning Newman never relaxes his view of his European experience as a holiday. He interrupts his stay in Paris to tour Europe, an excursion which dramatizes Newman's moral inadequacy for his approaching personal involvement with European values. Newman, tastelessly and greedily, tries to take as much of Europe with him as he can; yet he is perfectly content with himself: he has no desire to emerge a European. Indeed, he superimposes the American values of efficiency and materialism upon everything he sees.

Newman meets the Reverend Benjamin Babcock, an arch representative of the New England conscience, and travels with him for several months. James uses the absurd Babcock to illuminate a serious deficiency in Newman. Newman "liked everything, he accepted everything, he found amusement in everything; he was not discriminating, his values were as vague and loose as if he had carried them in his trousers pocket" (II, 91). Babcock, on the other hand, "detested Europe and felt an irritated need to protest against Newman's easy homage to so compromised a charmer. . . . He mistrusted the 'European' temperament. . . . 'European' life seemed to him unscrupulous and impure" (II, 92). Babcock has in excess the very qualities which Newman lacks: responsibility and restraint. The two Americans are alike, however, in their innocence, for neither is prepared to face the decadence of Europe.

Newman's inability to recognize evil is a steady motif in the novel. "Isn't [Claire], as a married woman, her own mistress?" (II, 109) he asks Mrs. Tristram when he learns of the authority the Bellegardes assume over her. When he hears more about Claire's forced marriage, he remarks, "It's like something in a regular old play" (II, 111), and asks, "Is it possible . . . that they can do this sort of thing over here?" (II, 111). Not until the end does he learn to take the evil of the Bellegardes seriously as a part

of the world in which he lives. Up to that point he oversimplifies
and underestimates his antagonists: "What should I be afraid of?
You can't hurt me unless you kill me by some violent means" (II,
303), Newman tells Valentin, with characteristic naïveté. Even
when he is wronged by the Bellegardes, he does not comprehend the meaning of their crime against him:

> And to be turned off because one was a commercial per-
> son! As if he had ever talked or dreamed of the commercial
> since his connexion with the Bellegardes began. . . .
> Granted one's being commercial was fair ground for one's
> being cleverly "sold," how little they knew about the class
> so designated and its enterprising way of not standing upon
> trifles (II, 421).

Newman makes the mistake of considering the Bellegardes' evil
as somehow to be explained rationally—either as a mistake or a
"trick."

When Newman learns from Mrs. Bread of the murder which
the Bellegardes have committed, he realizes the gravity of the evil
he is dealing with. The murder explicitly relates bad manners to
bad morals. James permits the reader to discover with Newman
that the surface capriciousness of the Bellegardes is in fact linked
with an evil that is invincible and incomprehensible (to the very
end Newman cannot fully understand the motivation and meaning of the Bellegardes; he can only accept them as a fact).

James does not define the evil of the Bellegardes—much of
their malignity depends on their mystery—but he describes it in
several ways. There is but limited effectiveness in the horror of
the family curse and the Gothic murder; nor is much gained by
the imagery of darkness, coldness, and complexity which suggests the miasma that surrounds the Bellegardes in both time and
space. James conveys the evil of the Bellegardes most effectively
through dramatic action. He establishes the connection between
the depravity and the aristocratic tradition of the family more
through Valentin and Claire, the morally superior Bellegardes,
than through the obvious villains, Mme. de Bellegarde and Urbain. When Valentin dies defending his honor—killed by a Ger-

man brewer in a duel caused by a dispute over a worthless co-
quette—the ugliness of family pride is forcefully conveyed. This
subordination of sense to an archaic notion of honor is "unnatural
and monstrous" (II, 388) to Newman, and clearly James is in
agreement.

When Claire quietly acquiesces to the will of her mother and
brother, she demonstrates her acceptance of their guilt:

> "I ought to have convinced you [she tells Newman] that I
> was doomed to disappoint you. But I *was*, in a way, too
> proud. . . . I'm too proud to be honest. . . . I'm afraid of
> being uncomfortable. . . . It's not marrying you; it's doing
> all that would go with it. It's the rupture, the defiance, the
> insisting upon being happy in my own way. What right have
> I to be happy when . . . others have so suffered?" (II,
> 411–412).

Newman, of course, cannot understand that Claire is by birth implicated in the evil of her family and must atone by renouncing
Newman and the freedom he proposes.

The traditional code of the European has the maturity and wisdom of age just as it has the evil which James usually associates
with age, for it holds as a first premise that a belief in happiness is
fallacious. To the Bellegardes personal contentment is neither a
desirable nor an attainable goal. Claire's mother and brother reject
the easy comfort of Newman's millions because they cannot
reconcile the source of the money with family honor. Newman
cannot comprehend Claire's renunciation, for he, till the conclusion of his experience, believes happiness to be the primary goal
in life. When Newman burns the note that would give him revenge, he reveals his maturity—he recognizes the superior value
of endurance; he denies himself the right to happiness through
self-assertion; and he realizes that evil is irremediable. Newman
has invaded Europe to reap its treasures, but he leaves it with a
higher sense of ethical values, a code of life closer to stoicism
than his original hedonism, and a knowledge of evil. In Newman's
case this knowledge produces a fineness of response that counter-
balances the anguish of humiliation and loss.

THE PORTRAIT OF A LADY

Like the other American heroines in James, Isabel Archer of
The Portrait of a Lady (1881), an enormous self-seeker who believes that reality corresponds to her ideals, whose innocence is
her strength as well as her weakness, is doomed to failure. James
repeatedly dramatizes the inadequacy of romance as a guide to
life.[30] He consistently shows the impossibility of complete success
for his Newmans, Euphemia Cleves, and Isabel Archers, and permits them to achieve only equivocal moral triumphs through endurance of suffering. Isabel Archer's history assumes this pattern,
but in *The Portrait of a Lady* James also treats a number of more
commonplace marriages. There is the marriage of the expatriates
Mr. and Mrs. Touchett, two different American types whose
marriage is all but a total failure. Mr. Touchett preserves the quiet
and honest dignity of his American nature in his English estate,
while his wife is quick to seek European values and friends. There
is the adulterous tie between the other expatriates, Osmond and
Mme. Merle. There is the marriage of the American Henrietta
and the English Bantling, both comic figures, whose union is an
ironic counterpart to Isabel's, for it gives all indications of being
the only successful marriage in the book. The marriage of Edward Rosier and Pansy Osmond is thwarted by Osmond. Ralph
Touchett, clearly in love with Isabel, is confined to the role of a
spectator by his illness. Finally, there is the Countess Gemini,
Osmond's sister, who has left America in her youth and married
a third-rate Italian nobleman. Her marriage is more or less in the
background of the novel, but it casts a grim shadow over the
proceedings in the foreground, for the Count Gemini is an im-
poverished gambler and the Countess has become an adulteress.

The marriage of Henrietta and Bantling is the only successful
one, and this seems to be mainly a comic contrast to the failure
of the others. The marriages not prevented by circumstances or
intervention end in futility or disaster. James's meaning is that
though theoretically the union of America—which represents
morality, innocence, and spirit—with Europe—which represents
manners, experience, and form—is an ideal arrangement, in actuality it can mean only misery. James recurrently explored the

possibilities of a workable union of America and Europe. Perhaps Felix Young of *The Europeans* embodies this ideal synthesis, but Young is the only character of his type in James's fiction. He is somewhat like Valentin Bellegarde of *The American*, yet Valentin is too intimately associated with the traditional values of his country to realize the freedom he desires. F. R. Leavis maintains that Ralph Touchett

> is the centre, the key-figure, of James's 'system'—the poise of harmony. . . . He is neither American nor English—or he is both: that is, he combines the advantages, while being free from the limitations. He can place everyone, and represents the ideal civilization that James found in no country.[31]

What Leavis overlooks is that Touchett is a ruined man. His incurable illness, which associates him with those Americans who are denied experience by physical, economic, or other handicaps, symbolizes impotence. Touchett can live only vicariously; he is, in effect, outside the action of the novel. More important, as Elizabeth Stevenson points out, "his living and dying as he does is a kind of reference to reality for Isabel." [32] Like Mercutio in *Romeo and Juliet* or Angela and the Beadsman in "The Eve of Saint Agnes," he is a kind of *memento mori*.

The failure of every marriage except Henrietta's also points to James's abiding conviction that isolation is the ultimate lot of every man. Social existence precludes love, friendship, and sympathy. The James character requires completion, and, just as *The Portrait of a Lady* illustrates the limitations of Isabel and Osmond by contrasting them, it stresses the futility of any attempt at a reconciliation of opposite qualities. At best—as in the case of Isabel and Warburton—there is no alteration in either person; at worst—as in the case of Isabel and Osmond—one person's deficiency injures the other. The morally superior person is thus driven further back into himself, forced to rely on his innate strength, forever estranged from a significant social relationship.

There is clearly a revelation of an intrinsic evil in the novel's emphasis on man's inevitable conditions of isolation and failure. But in *The Portrait* James is also concerned with the process of man's decline from innocence to depravity. Nearly all James's novels treat to some extent the theme of the Fall of Man—the single theme which dominated so much of nineteenth-century American literature—but no one work so explicitly as *The Portrait of a Lady*.

In James's version of the Fall myth America is Eden. As Felix Young says of the society of the Wentworths in *The Europeans*, "It's primitive; it's patriarchal; it's the *ton* of the golden age." [33] The idyllic American paradise suits the moral innocence of the Americans. The innocents leave their paradise of their own will. If they are expelled from Eden, the force is their own selfhood, a pride which urges them to master experience. In spite of the language of Emersonian transcendentalism with which James's Americans consider their goals, they are clearly motivated by an unhealthy egotism. Isabel, for example,

> had an unquenchable desire to think well of herself. She had a theory that it was only under this provision life was worth living; that one should be one of the best, should be conscious of a fine organization (she couldn't help knowing her organization was fine), should move in a realm of light, of natural wisdom, of happy impulse, of inspiration gracefully chronic. . . . She spent half her time in thinking of beauty and bravery and magnanimity; she had a fixed determination to regard the world as a place of brightness, of free expansion, or irresistible action . . . (III, 68).

Such pride, based on a belief in the goodness and possibility of unlimited emotional and intellectual expansion, is also an active aggressiveness that can easily become evil. What distinguishes the Americans and the Europeans in *The Portrait of a Lady* is that the Americans are ambitious to possess something or someone. In this sense, the aims of Isabel and Osmond are similar, for both wish to satisfy their own cravings. But Isabel's pride is untainted by malice; rather it stems from her "meagre knowledge, her inflated ideals, her confidence at once innocent and dogmatic" (III, 69). When Isabel leaves the Edenlike America, she seeks a total knowledge and freedom; disillusion comes with the awareness that the two are mutually exclusive. As Leon Edel points out, "twice in the book James uses Miltonic words to describe the extent of Isabel's freedom—as if she were Eve standing at the portals of Paradise, which are closing behind her." [34] Though Isabel is more innocent than Eve at the beginning of her adventure, her innocence is ambiguous; it combines a false notion of personal independence with an obliviousness to evil. In this sense her original sin is simply innocence, but an innocence coordinate with pride.

It is significant that *The Portrait of a Lady* concludes with Goodwood offering Isabel a way out of her misery:

"It's too monstrous of you to think of sinking back into that misery, of going to open your mouth to that poisoned air. . . . Why shouldn't we be happy—when it's here before us, when it's so easy? . . . We can do absolutely as we please. . . . Were we born to rot in our misery? . . . The world's all before us—and the world's very big. I know something about that" (IV, 434–435).

The point is that Goodwood knows nothing about the world, for his pleas recall the former beliefs of Isabel, who at this point has so matured through her contact with evil that she can reply, "The world's very small" (IV, 435). Goodwood proposes an enormous temptation, as only now does Isabel realize the worth of the happiness that Goodwood offers: "She had wanted help, and here was help; it had come in a rushing torrent" (IV, 435). Isabel's renunciation of escape from Osmond and of happiness with Goodwood is a triumph of her (and James's) idealism; it avows the supreme dignity of the human being. James does nothing to minimize the suffering with which Isabel must spend the rest of her life, but he suggests that the acquired wisdom, the expansion of consciousness, represents a development far higher not only than her life in America but higher than her life with Warburton or Goodwood would have been. When Isabel partakes of the Tree of Knowledge in the world of experience she is made forcefully aware of the presence of evil, but in a sense her earlier ambitions are fulfilled. She was perhaps correct in pursuing her ideals, in accepting nothing but the fullest experiences that life can offer.

From the beginning Isabel vaguely realizes that her restlessness
for knowledge will not be satisfied until she faces evil. When she
tells Ralph, ". . . I don't wish to touch the cup of experience.
It's a poisoned drink! I only want to see for myself" (III, 213)
(echoing Rowland Mallet), she speaks of impossibilities, and
Ralph spots the flaw in her wish: "You want to see, but not to feel"
(III, 213). But for the most part Isabel's quest is far from superficial; she tells Warburton after rejecting his proposal, "I can't
escape unhappiness. . . . In marrying you I shall be trying to"
(III, 186). Here Isabel knows unhappiness only abstractly, but
she realizes that she must experience it to fulfill her mission. On
several occasions she asks Ralph to show her the ghost of Gardencourt. Ralph's reply to her first request is significant:

> Ralph shook his head sadly. "I might show it to you, but
> you'd never see it. The privilege isn't given to every one;
> it's not enviable. It has never been seen by a young, happy,
> innocent person like you. You must have suffered first, have
> suffered greatly, have gained some miserable knowledge. In
> that way your eyes are opened to it. I saw it long ago," said
> Ralph.
> "I told you just now I'm very fond of knowledge," Isabel
> answered.
> "Yes, of happy knowledge—of pleasant knowledge. But
> you haven't suffered, and you're not made to suffer. I hope
> you'll never see the ghost" (III, 64).

This is light banter, but it serves to point up a serious shortcoming in Isabel: she wants a total knowledge, including a knowledge of evil, but cannot recognize that an association with evil
will require her to compromise her enormous goals.

Knowledge, especially a knowledge of evil, proves to be a
recompense for sorrow. The Fall of Man is basically (i.e., morally) fortunate because through experience Isabel loses the characteristics of her innocence which caused her to be ignorant and
proud, to believe that she could exercise an unlimited freedom in
the world. Through experience she is enabled to realize the finer
qualities of her innocence—a sense of decency, a generosity of
spirit, a capacity to give—and she has learned the great lesson

that one should neither renounce his ideals nor make life conform to them, that the ultimate achievement in life is the preservation of the integrity of the human character. For, after all, Isabel is the winner in the end; by accepting Goodwood's offer she would in effect be rejecting her freedom, her belief in the value of her own decision.

In spite of the European setting, *The Portrait of a Lady* is mainly about America. James takes a gallery of American types, removes them from the limited American environment, in which they have no opportunity to change, and places them in Europe, where they are free to indulge in the fine art of living and susceptible to experience that tests their moral stability. Caspar Goodwood and Henrietta Stackpole are closed from experience by their protective Americanism; both distrust Europe and refuse to recognize its advantages over America. Ralph Touchett and Mr. Touchett are more sensitive; yet they neither assimilate European values nor reject them, for they are destined to inactivity, Ralph by his illness and his father by his business and his age. Edward Rosier, the thwarted lover of Pansy, is of little importance in himself as his function is mainly technical. Generally, however, his response to Europe is limited to an appreciation of its art. The other expatriates, except Isabel, repudiate America entirely and fully accept European standards of conduct. Mrs. Touchett, Gilbert Osmond, Mme. Merle, and the Countess Gemini are outstanding examples of the thoroughly Europeanized American.

Mrs. Touchett is neither good nor evil. Yet she represents negatively the defects of Europe and its injurious effects on the American. She is in many ways like the American women who persecute Daisy Miller; she resembles Osmond and Mme. Merle in her total devotion to forms and convention. But with Mrs. Touchett—and unlike Mme. Merle and Osmond—the polished surface does not disguise an inner evil. Rather it covers a kind of emptiness, an emotional vacuum. At the deaths of her husband and her son, she is repellingly unfeeling. After Ralph's death she "appeared to be absorbed in considering, without enthusiasm but with perfect lucidity, the new conveniences of her own situation"

(IV, 422). Mrs. Touchett's cool rationality leads Isabel to wonder if her aunt "were not even missing those enrichments of consciousness and privately trying—reaching out for some aftertaste of life, dregs of the banquet; the testimony of pain or the cold recreation of remorse" (IV, 406–407). James's Americans are most often heart characters: they readily respond to intuitions and feelings. But in *The Portrait of a Lady* Mrs. Touchett and the other long-time expatriates are almost completely head characters. It is as if their excessive devotion to manners has dried up all feeling.

Also Mrs. Touchett is a rover. She is rootless and unattached, aloof from her son and husband and devoted to travelling. She is a seeker of culture and manners who is content to remain on the surface of life. Though her ideal is more realistic than Isabel's —she seeks the attainable—it is also more superficial and less valuable, for Isabel, to misuse Henrietta Stackpole's phrase, is interested in "the inner life," a knowledge of more than forms.

The combined characteristics of formalism, rootlessness, and rationalism are most evident in Mme. Merle and Osmond. These two, however, are incontestably evil. Their capacity for evil is partly explained by their nationality. The American is capable of a greater malignity than the European because of his freedom. Furthermore, as F. W. Dupee observes, the Americans are all self-seekers,[35] aggressive in their plunder of Europe. The Europeans—characters like Richard de Mauves and Urbain de Bellegarde—are conservatives who resort to evil to preserve their old values and possessions. More often than not, their sins are sins of exclusion; they betray not in an effort to gain, but in a refusal to give.

The significant difference between Isabel and Osmond is that when Isabel realizes that her demands on life are exorbitant she withdraws; Isabel learns through experience that unrestrained acquisitiveness—emotional, intellectual, or material—is inconsistent with her high moral code, as she learns that her duty is to give rather than to receive. Osmond, on the other hand, employs his refined awareness of the complexities of life to further his self-seeking ends. To put it somewhat differently, Isabel's knowledge of the world is complemented by self-knowledge, so that her

ultimate awareness is one of moral as well as social truth, whereas
Osmond's is solely of social truth.

Osmond and Isabel also differ in their ways of knowing. Isabel
responds to experience emotionally and spontaneously, eventually
replacing all her dangerous abstract beliefs about freedom, experience, and happiness by a kind of pragmatic insight, an expe-
riential grasp of what is real and of what is right. "I've only one
ambition," Isabel says, "to be free to follow out a good feeling"
(IV, 73). In complete contrast, Osmond lives in a world governed
by impersonal ideas. Osmond's manner derives from his conception of what it should be; it accords with a social rather than
a personal ideal. His conduct is from beginning to end totally
calculated, from his initial project to ensnare Isabel to his posture
when he forbids Isabel to visit the dying Ralph. Negatively
Osmond's coldly intelligent manner—similar to that of the Hawthorne villain, especially Chillingworth and Rappacini—is revealed in the absence of love and sympathy in his dealings with
those who are most intimate with him: with Isabel, whom he
marries for money; with his daughter, whose love for Edward
Rosier he suppresses; with his one-time mistress, Mme. Merle,
whom he uses as a piece of machinery to better his position.
Positively, Osmond's narrow but keen intellect is revealed in his
shrewd operations to gain Isabel's favor. There is a special horror
in his calculated abuse of Isabel's feelings; Osmond knows emotions only abstractly, but he knows them well. Stephen Spender
has noted that in *The American* evil is "Elizabethan in its mech-
anism"; [36] and in *The Portrait of a Lady* Osmond suggests Iago.
His conquest of Isabel is intrigue in its purest form. Like Iago
Osmond sets a series of traps and carefully plans his approach.
After Osmond and Mme. Merle prearrange the marriage behind
Isabel's back, each works separately to carry out the plan. The
strategy is brilliant: Mme. Merle advises Isabel that the Countess
Gemini is a habitual liar, thus nullifying the Countess' own
strength, for the latter knows of the previous liaison between
Mme. Merle and Osmond, and Mme. Merle fears that she may
tell Isabel; Osmond arranges for Isabel to visit Pansy in Florence,
well knowing that his daughter's innocent charm will captivate
Isabel and influence her towards him. Isabel is completely fooled.

Rarely in James—Maggie Verver is possibly the only exception—is there a complete balance between the head and the heart. The good are duped by the worldly-wise, who in turn lack the instinctive charity of the good. When one combines these virtues —as does Ralph Touchett—he is compelled to remain outside the story as a kind of chorus.

Gilbert Osmond's formalism is a paradoxical kind of egotism. More than anyone else in the book he stands for the impersonal values of tradition, convention, and society. Isabel Archer, for all her self-esteem, is no match for Osmond as an egotist. In his devotion to convention he has a hostility to freedom; his byword is exclusion. He marries Isabel not just to get her money, but to bend her spirit, to possess her heart and mind. "The real offence, as she ultimately perceived, was her having a mind of her own at all. Her mind was to be his—attached to his own like a small garden-plot to a deer-park" (IV, 200). Not only is Osmond repelled by Isabel's independence, but he wishes to subjugate her as he has subjugated himself to convention. Osmond wishes to possess art, tradition, and manners: for him they are not attributes of a meaningful and well regulated society but matters to be appropriated exclusively as his own. His interest in art is especially perverse, for, unlike Edward Rosier, also a collector, who sells his valuable possessions out of love for Pansy, Osmond collects treasures for the sake of owning them and making it impossible for others to own them. As Joseph J. Firebaugh observes, "Isabel comes to realize that he values beauty, not as a mode of knowledge of human life, but as a symbol of traditional power and inherited wealth." [37] He has made an unnatural distinction between aesthetic values and human values: "He's the incarnation of taste," Ralph Touchett observes. "He judges and measures, approves and condemns, altogether by that" (IV, 71). Just as Osmond's conduct and speech are perfect representations of traditional manners, his physical presence is hardly distinguishable from the works of art that surround him. When he accuses Isabel of treachery as she asks his permission to visit Ralph at his deathbed, Osmond is characteristically engaged in copying an antique coin.

But for all of Osmond's veneer, he is ultimately revealed as common. The gravity of his evil is obvious from its contagious effects on Isabel and Pansy, and even on Mme. Merle and Edward Rosier. Its grossness is also apparent, however, in his brutal control of Isabel. When he drops the veil of cultivation and speaks from his nature, the superficiality of his refinement becomes clear. Towards the end of the book, when Isabel learns the full truth, she finds that beneath Osmond's sophistication is the sordidness of an adulterous connection with Mme. Merle and that Osmond's supposed superiority to normal human desires is a fiction: "She found herself confronted . . . with the conviction that the man in the world whom she had supposed to be the least sordid had married her, like a vulgar adventurer, for her money" (IV, 330). Contrasted with the elegance of Osmond and Mme. Merle, the Countess Gemini's exposure of them gains added force, for beneath the glamorous surface we find only the coarsest of animal impulses. Osmond insults Isabel in their final meeting with particular crudity; also he ridicules Caspar Goodwood in an act of gratuitous malice. At the end there is little doubt that Osmond's celebrated superiority is meretricious.

The Countess Gemini and Mme. Merle are also mainly characters of surface. "The Countess seemed [to Isabel] to have no soul; she was like a bright rare shell, with a polished surface and a remarkably pink lip, in which something would rattle when you shook it" (IV, 225–226). The Countess represents an extreme decadence, the result of a lifetime of sterile existence in a corrupt society. She is neither good nor evil; she resides in the background of the story, aware of the sins of the past but incapable of redeeming the present. She does not tell Isabel the truth about Osmond and Mme. Merle until it can only make Isabel's pain even greater.

Mme. Merle resembles the Countess in her hollowness. As with Mrs. Touchett, "Emotion . . . had become with [Mme. Merle] rather historic; she made no secret of the fact that the fount of passion, thanks to having been rather violently tapped at one period, didn't flow quite so freely as of yore" (III, 268). Later she makes it clear that the source of her coldness is Osmond: "You've not only dried up my tears; you've dried up my soul" (IV, 334), she tells him. Aside from Osmond's responsibility for her cor-

ruption, other factors tend to modify her evil. For she is at least
partly motivated in her deception of Isabel by a regard for her
daughter, Pansy: she knows not only that Isabel's money will
enable Pansy to marry well, but also that Isabel's influence will
counterweight Osmond's. Mme. Merle has nothing to gain from
her part in the intrigue. Most important, she is finally, like Lady
Macbeth, overcome with guilt. In her final scene with Osmond,
she alone accepts guilt and renounces any further implication in
their mutual crime. "I don't know how we're to end. I wish I
did! How do bad people end?—especially as to their *common*
crimes. You have made me as bad as yourself" (IV, 335). Mme.
Merle ends by going to America to accept a kind of penance, an
atonement for the evil of the past. Nonetheless, Mme. Merle is a
creature of free will; no extenuating circumstances can lessen her
guilt. Her perception of her own baseness indicates not that she
is saved, but that she is damned—and that she knows it.

   As Osmond lives for art, Mme. Merle lives for society. "She's
the great round world itself!" (III, 362). She lives "exclusively
for the world" (IV, 144). A creature of brilliant surface, she has
achieved a state of social completeness. Ralph Touchett says that
Mme. Merle "pushes the search for perfection too far—that her
merits are in themselves overstrained. She's too good, too kind,
too clever, too learned, too accomplished, too everything. She's
too complete, in a word" (III, 361). Isabel's analysis of her friend
is also acute:

   If for Isabel she had a fault it was that she was not natural;
   . . . her nature had been too much overlaid by custom and
   her angles too much rubbed away. She had become too
   flexible, too useful, was too ripe and too final. She was in a
   word too perfectly the social animal that man and woman
   are supposed to have been intended to be; and she had rid
   herself of every remnant of that tonic wildness which we
   may assume to have belonged even to the most amiable persons in the ages before countryhouse life was the fashion.
   Isabel found it difficult to think of her in any detachment or
   privacy, she existed only in her relations, direct or indirect,
   with her fellow mortals (III, 273–274).

Mme. Merle has the same distrust of personal resources that Osmond has; she is a slave to propriety. In a crucial passage Mme. Merle remarks to Isabel that no one is important in himself but in "the whole envelope of circumstances. There's no such thing as an isolated man or woman; we're each of us made up of some cluster of appurtenances" (III, 287). In Mme. Merle's belief that man is entirely a social animal, she is sharply contrasted to Isabel, who modifies but never rejects her belief in the supreme value of personal resources: "Nothing that belongs to me is any measure of me; everything's on the contrary a limit, a barrier, and a perfectly arbitrary one" (III, 288). Like Emerson and Thoreau before him, James holds that evil consists in adopting the world's values before one's own. For Mme. Merle's devotion to the ways of the world necessarily involves her repudiation of the moral sense, which transcends convention and external systems. The James character must find his salvation by retaining and exercising his natural moral faculty in an environment which emphasizes the unnatural social values. Obviously Mme. Merle and Gilbert Osmond have sacrificed their richest American trait in order to participate in the ambiguous glory of Europe.

CHAPTER THREE

Evil in London

THE INEFFECTUAL HERO

THE PRINCESS CASAMASSIMA (1886) is a bridge between the international fiction of the eighties and the London novels of the nineties. James has switched the scene from the European continent to London, the hero's nationality from American to British, and his economic condition from wealth to poverty. But the basic elements of his character and adventure are the same: the intelligent and imaginative person is introduced to a world of culture and wealth which takes him into its confidence and then betrays him. James's major alteration in *The Princess Casamassima* and most of his novels of the next fifteen years is to diminish the stature of the hero. He is not only poor, but he is also powerless. Unlike the Americans who invade Europe with dynamic vigor and confidence, the heroes of the London novels are armed only with their sensibilities.

Christopher Newman and Isabel Archer are allowed an initial triumph before encountering disaster, but the London hero makes no progress; he is thwarted from the beginning. Isabel gains a qualified victory over her antagonists. Her innate charm, dignity, and intelligence contrast favorably with the acquired finesse of the expatriate Americans. Her moral superiority to Mrs. Touchett, Mme. Merle, and Gilbert Osmond is unequivocal. She loses happiness, but she acquires spiritual nobility. After Isabel, James's heroes and heroines become progressively less attractive, so that with "The Turn of the Screw" and *The Sacred Fount* they become as perverse and grotesque as their adversaries.

In James's fiction of the 1890's, goodness reaches its nadir.

56

If good is ineffective and subject to treachery in *The Portrait of a Lady*, it is nevertheless accorded dignity. But in *The Princess Casamassima*, where there is only Hyacinth Robinson (unless we count the inept Mrs. Pynsent and Mr. Vetch) to uphold the moral sense in a corrupt world, there are no characters equivalent to Ralph Touchett, Henrietta Stackpole, Pansy Osmond, and Caspar Goodwood, individuals who, though they do not offset the evil of Osmond and Mme. Merle, present a formidable array of private virtue. Also isolated in a world of various shades of egotism, Fleda Vetch of *The Spoils of Poynton* (1897) has only the "pointlessly active and pleasantly dull" (X, 9) Owen Gereth as an ally. Mrs. Gereth and Mona Brigstock possess all the force.

It is especially significant that in *The Spoils of Poynton* virtue itself is not entirely admirable, as it is in *The Portrait of a Lady*. Fleda's virtue is so incongruous with the society in which she exercises it that the effect is to make her seem overscrupulous, perhaps even ridiculous. Mrs. Gereth tells Fleda, "[I] fail to comprehend the inanity of a passion that bewilders a young blockhead [Owen] with bugaboo barriers, with hideous and monstrous sacrifices. I can only repeat that you're beyond me. Your perversity's a thing to howl over" (X, 225). Mrs. Gereth, whose uncompromising practicality is as immoral in its way as Mona Brigstock's greed, certainly does not speak for James, nor does James give any indication that he doubts the validity of the private conscience. But nowhere in *The Portrait of a Lady* does Isabel Archer appear so foolish as Fleda Vetch. It may simply be that Isabel's problems are far weightier than Fleda's, as are her ambitions and adventures, so that delicate moral discrimination is necessary for her situation. In *The Spoils of Poynton* Mrs. Gereth's ridicule of Fleda is in many ways paralleled by the dramatic action of the novel. In a European society based on tradition and manners, Isabel adheres to the accepted code by refusing to repudiate Osmond. The world of *The Spoils of Poynton* is the modern world, where tradition gives way to expediency and customs support passions. Thus Fleda's insistence on the old rules strikes Mrs. Gereth as out of date and Mona Brigstock as absurd.

The American hero of the early international fiction is young, successful, sensitive, and intelligent. Because of his ignorance of the ways of the world, he is deceived and betrayed. But in his state of innocence he is magnanimous, and in his state of experience he gains an inner strength through full awareness. The hero of James's middle period is unsuccessful from the beginning of his life. He is also unattractive. Even when exercising the moral sense he is likely to be self-consciously priggish. Thus Fleda Vetch, with a kind of pride singularly absent in Newman and Isabel Archer, decides to renounce marriage to Owen and possession of the spoils:

> Nothing was really straight but to justify her little pensioned presence by her use; and now, won over as she was to heroism, she could see her use only as some high and delicate deed. She couldn't in short do anything at all unless she could do it with a degree of pride, and there would be nothing to be proud of in having arranged for poor Owen to get off easily (X, 106).

At this point Fleda's act of pride, especially from Mrs. Gereth's point of view, is extremely perverse, for Fleda betrays the kindness shown to her by directly counteracting her benefactress's plans.

In the novels from *The Spoils of Poynton* to *The Awkward Age*, moral refinement appears at times as a kind of immorality in itself. That is, renunciation of happiness is no longer a purely personal matter, as it is for Newman and Isabel. Since the London heroes are less free from restricting circumstances than their predecessors, their acts of self-denial affect others as well as themselves. To renounce Owen, Fleda must necessarily betray Mrs. Gereth; to renounce Sir Claude, Maisie must distress Mrs. Wix.

In his middle period James is refocusing his picture of the individual and the world, so that the opposition between the two loses its clarity. In other words, James has revised his conception of moral reality: in appearance good and evil are not clearly distinct; good is so weak and incongruous with its environment that it may seem grotesque; the honorable man is objectively perverse and queer. Moreover, moral conduct often necessitates the violation of inadequate, if not false, moral systems recognized

by society. To try to reconcile the demands of conscience with
those of society—to be moral in an immoral world—may cause
one to become corrupted himself. Thus there exists an utter
inversion of moral conduct: good may appear evil and evil may
appear good. Because modern social existence is based on false
principles, it is often necessary to be false regardless of motive
and intention.

Thus, in *The Spoils of Poynton*, Fleda Vetch must appear
freakish, even perhaps mad, in her extreme scrupulosity. To do
less than she does—to accept Mrs. Gereth's bribe, to allow Owen
to break his pledge to Mona—would be to accept Mrs. Gereth's
utilitarian values as her own. But for Fleda to do the opposite—
to adhere to a superior code which she knows to be right—she
must, first, betray the confidence Mrs. Gereth has placed in her,
and, second, tell a direct lie. Mrs. Gereth, of course, places Fleda
in the awkward position of having to appear ungrateful and of
having to lie, because it is she who commits the initial crime of
adopting Fleda for her deceitful purposes: she frankly "uses"
Fleda to lure Owen away from Mona. Having gratefully accepted
Mrs. Gereth's seemingly innocent proposal that she live with her,
Fleda, in order to remain free from complicity in her benefactress's plot, must necessarily refuse to cooperate. Correspondingly, Fleda must lie to Mrs. Gereth—must falsify what she
knows to be true, that Mona Brigstock will not marry Owen
unless Mrs. Gereth returns the treasures to Poynton—in order to
prevent her from refusing to return the spoils and disrupting the
marriage. When she learns of Mona's decision from Owen, Fleda
is fully conscious of the curious position she is in:

> If she should now repeat his words this wouldn't at all play
> the game of her definite vow; it would only play the game of
> her little gagged and blinded desire. She could calculate well
> enough the result of telling Mrs. Gereth, how she had had it
> from Owen's troubled lips that Mona was only waiting for
> the restitution and would do nothing without it. The thing
> was to obtain the restitution without imparting that knowl-
> edge. The only way also not to impart it was not to tell any
> truth at all about it; and the only way to meet this last condi-

tion was to reply to her companion as she presently did. "He
told me nothing whatever. He didn't touch on the subject"
(X, 119–120).

A fundamental trait of Fleda is her alienation from human
society—a common limitation with James's middle period heroines. Fleda is clothed only with an idea, Mrs. Gereth thinks, and
the novel shows her to be one of James's typical seeking heroines,
with a large appetite for experience. Her imagination, her re-
sponsiveness to art and society, along with her deep moral sense,
align her with Isabel Archer, Milly Theale, and a dozen other
"heiresses of all the ages." She shares, however, the particular
limitations of the English protagonist of the middle period in that
she is sealed off in a tightly restricted society—by poverty, by
friendlessness, and mainly by the impersonality and dense materialism of London itself.

There is a spectrum of intelligences in *The Spoils of Poynton*.
At the lowest point is the absolute willfulness of Mona Brigstock.
Mona sees only that the furniture and art objects of Poynton—
to her more than anyone they are "spoils"—are valuable: they
must be, since Mrs. Gereth regards them highly and they have
been praised in the society columns. Mrs. Gereth herself has a
fine aesthetic awareness, which places her above Mona; but the
action finally reveals her to be more like Mona than like Fleda:
she sees only what she wants. She has taste—she knows why the
spoils are valuable; and she is clever—she has gotten them at the
best prices; also she is ingenious in devising ways to prevent Mona
from getting them. But in the final analysis, she has perversely
subordinated intelligence to will. Owen Gereth is a kind of *tabula
rasa:* neither will nor thought directs him; and thus he is mani-
festly weak, the easy tool of the three women in his life. Repeatedly seen in images of the natural man, he acts through casual
instincts only. Finally, Fleda herself has maximum—though certainly incomplete—awareness. Her appreciation for the art objects and splendid trappings of Poynton is not a compartmental-
ized activity of the mind; rather it is the same grasp of reality
that presents her with moral scruples.

It is not farfetched to say that *The Spoils of Poynton* dramatizes the position of *logos*—or contemplation—in a world of *ethos* —or action. The characters who act do so blindly; thus the one person who thinks is prohibited from action. Through a series of almost maddening moral dilemmas, the novel leads Fleda to the point of moral anarchy, where the very terms of her principles have been obscured, converted, and rendered all but meaningless.

Fleda's isolation from social intercourse of any sort is only gradually revealed, but it is her condition from the start of the book. One wonders how she was ever invited to Waterbath, where Mrs. Gereth first meets her, since she seems to be on close terms with no one other than her pitiful father and newly married sister. In any event, Mrs. Gereth, in the familiar role of Jamesian fairy godmother, impresses Fleda with what seems a kindred sensitivity to beauty, and shortly afterwards attempts to manipulate Fleda into attracting Owen away from Mona. The book rapidly shows Fleda accepting two—mutually contradictory—loyalties: to Mrs. Gereth, who has taken her to Poynton and befriended her; and to Owen, who in his simplicity asks Fleda to "bring Mommy around" to accepting Mona. Separate from these loyalties, which become increasingly more demanding and involving, is Fleda's own notion, strong from the beginning, that Owen cannot in honor ignore his pledge to Mona. Fleda, of course, is thoroughly involved in Mrs. Gereth's life, both in her intrigue to keep the spoils from falling to Mona, and in her charm, grace, and taste. She has unwittingly committed herself to Mrs. Gereth and more knowingly committed herself to Owen, whose position she alone sees to be a moral one.

Once involved in Mrs. Gereth's schemes, Fleda, quite literally, cannot escape; and she frequently tries. The pattern of the novel is that of Fleda's withdrawing and being brought back by one or the other of the Gereths, each urging her to align herself against the other. She is also, of course, partly restrained from complete withdrawal by her growing love for Owen, her sensibility to Poynton, and her fondness for Mrs. Gereth. Thus, after she realizes that Mrs. Gereth is using her as bait to lure Owen from Mona, Fleda feels that "she couldn't possibly remain after being offered to Owen" (X, 33). And yet she does—for a fortnight; and then she proceeds with Mrs. Gereth to Ricks. Back in her

father's house, she is again drawn to the Gereth affair by meeting
Owen in the street. However, it is only after Mrs. Gereth plun-
ders Poynton to stock Ricks that Fleda attempts to escape: she
shelters herself in her father's house. At this point James clearly
conveys Fleda's dilemma:

> She had neither a home nor an outlook—nothing in all the
> wide world but a feeling of suspense. . . . only a horrible
> sense of privation. She had quite moved from under Mrs.
> Gereth's wide wing; and now that she was really among the
> penwipers and ash-trays she was swept, at the thought of all
> the beauty she had forsworn, by short wild gusts of despair
> (X, 145).

At her father's, where she has determined to communicate with
neither Owen nor his mother, Fleda is visited, first by Owen, who
proposes marriage to her and urges that she allow him to break
off from Mona, and then by Mrs. Brigstock, who finds her in a
compromising meeting with Owen. When she again tries to escape—this time to her sister's house outside of London—she is
again pursued by Owen and also receives a telegram from Mrs.
Gereth urging Fleda to visit her. Significantly, the novel concludes with Fleda once more travelling, this time to Poynton,
where she sees only the black smoke of its destruction and the
end of everything.

Unlike those novels in which the journey motif provides a
structural symbol of a journey to knowledge, to liberation, or to
maturity, in *The Spoils of Poynton*, the withdrawal and return
pattern, accentuated by Fleda's homelessness and mixed feeling
toward the Gereths, comes to symbolize her unavoidable involvement in a world not of her own making.

When she leaves for her sister's, Fleda feels that

> She required for this step no reason but the sense of neces-
> sity. It was a strong personal need; she wished to interpose
> something, and there was nothing she could interpose but
> distance, but time. If Mrs. Brigstock had to deal with Owen
> she would allow Mrs. Brigstock the chance. To be there, to
> be in the midst of it, was the reverse of what she craved: she

had already been more in the midst of it than had ever entered into her plan. At any rate she had renounced her plan; she had no plan now but the plan of separation. This was to abandon Owen, to give up the fine office of helping him back to his own . . . (X, 179).

The renunciation is, of course, thwarted by Owen, just as it was he who previously had sought her out. Thus it is that Fleda's travels come to symbolize her undesired moral involvement in others' lives, her perilous passivity that must in the long run be converted to action. Fleda has the imagination of the free spirit, but is simply unable to remain free. To allow Owen to break his pledge to Mona is tantamount to ignoring the dictates of conscience by which she knows the dishonor of such an act. Nor can she leave Owen free to do what he wishes, for she is part of his plans. She must interfere with him, tell him he must honor his pledge, in order to avoid complicity. It should not be forgotten that the engagement is of Owen's and not of Fleda's making; it is not she who consigns him to a life of misery with Mona Brigstock. Fleda simply cannot be a part of the violation herself. It is Owen who repeatedly seeks her out, just as it is Mrs. Gereth who makes demands upon her. Fleda should be accused neither of interference in the lives of the Gereths, nor of narrow self-righteousness. She has really no alternative between a complete abandonment of scruples and a perverse, even incomprehensible, renunciation.

In less subtle stories than *The Spoils of Poynton*, James exposes the limitations of his middle-period protagonists through irony. Most of his London tales are told from the point of view of the protagonists, who consistently evaluate their own conduct as heroic and rarely suspect their own flaws. James's ironic treatment of his leading character is most apparent in "In the Cage" (1898), the story of a girl who works in a telegraph office, where she takes messages from the upper-class men and women of London's West End. Shut off from any rich experience of her own by poverty and a sterile personal life, she takes vicarious pleasure in handling the communications of her social superiors. There is a certain pathos in the girl's "spending, in framed and wired confinement, the life of a guinea-pig or magpie" (XI, 367), but her adolescent devotion to those who give her messages to send is not only juvenile but self-destructive. James makes this obvious in several ways: first, the girl cannot help but know from the implications of the communications she transmits that the people she admires are, as she herself says, "selfish brutes" (XI, 400), ostentatious in their lavish spending, unconcerned with the plight of the less fortunate, and primarily interested in their own illicit love affairs; secondly, because of her foolish loyalty to people who are hardly aware of her existence, the girl ignores her responsibility to Mr. Mudge, the substantial if unromantic grocer to whom she is engaged.

It is significant that James never reveals the girl's name. And, as with the anonymous narrators of "The Turn of the Screw" and *The Sacred Fount*, the point is that she really has no identity, for she exists not in herself, but only in others. Again a comparison with *The Portrait of a Lady* should clarify the alteration of the Jamesian protagonist. Isabel idealizes Europe, which she knows to offer a rich experience and believes to be no more immoral than her own America; the girl telegraphist idealizes West End society, which she knows to be permanently closed to her, which she knows to be immoral, and which offers no valuable experience. Likewise, Isabel's adventure in Europe is personal, whereas the telegraphist's adventure in the cage is vicarious. Isabel is fully committed to Gilbert Osmond; the telegraphist is engaged to Mr. Mudge and infatuated with Captain Everard.

The innocence of such American women as Euphemia Cleve and Isabel Archer manifests itself in their easy enchantment with Europe. Their stories record their progress from illusion to disillusion. The plots of "In the Cage" and "The Turn of the Screw" develop the same basic progression, but, with America replaced by London slums or country villages and the European aristocracy by a vulgar upper class, much of the objective beauty and meaning of the world is gone. Not even in the beginning is the reader's sympathy fully with the heroine as it is with Isabel, whose innocence and illusions are readily excused. In James's middle period, he frequently stresses the immaturity more than the incorruptibility of his innocent protagonists.

These are most often children or adolescents: Morgan Moreen of "The Pupil," Maisie Farange of *What Maisie Knew*, the telegraphist of "In the Cage," the governess and children of "The Turn of the Screw," and Nanda Brookenham of *The Awkward Age*. The child in these works has a definite ambivalence. James emphasizes both the innocence and the ignorance of his immaturity: when the child is passive he is helpless and pure; when he is active he is stupid and inept. On the one hand, James achieves a pathos foreign to his earlier international tales by exposing children to corruption. In a world defiled by adults, the child has little opportunity for spiritual expansion. He can only withdraw from the world into himself: to retreat from the cage with Mr. Mudge, to retreat from Sir Claude with Mrs. Wix, to retreat from Mrs. Brook with Mr. Longdon. To remain in the world too long is either to be destroyed by it, like Morgan Moreen, or to become an adult and therefore corrupt oneself, like Little Aggie of *The Awkward Age*.

When the burden of goodness is placed on the child the impossibility of its triumph is emphasized. When the children act in society their efforts are either misdirected or ineffectual. Maisie thinks she is doing everyone a service when she brings together Sir Claude and Mrs. Beale, but she is only a valuable, though innocent, means of aiding an evil she cannot possibly understand. The telegraphist, more naïve than her years would indicate, wishes to assist her beloved customer, Captain Everard, and, when she is able to recall the wording of an old telegram, enables him to avert a scandal. But such practical aid is no more commendable than that given by Maisie. Nanda Brookenham tries to protect Little Aggie from corruption, and persuades Mitchy to marry her. When the marriage fails—Aggie readily submits to adultery—Mitchy's distress is certainly Nanda's fault. In each of these cases, goodness, combined with ignorance, leads directly to evil.

A notable characteristic of much of James's work is the frequency with which characters offer to "save" others. In his middle period, James employs the theme of salvation ironically. He shows apparent good to conceal real evil. First, there are those whose supposedly charitable missions conceal the most malicious plans. In "The Middle Years" (1893), Miss Vernham demands that the novelist Dencombe leave Bournemouth, where he is convalescing from a serious illness, in order that his disciple, Doctor Hugh, may be free to return to his patient, the Countess. The Countess has taken a great liking to the doctor and given assurance of leaving him a fortune. Miss Vernham is in love with the doctor and feels that nothing should prevent him from getting the money. But the effect of the girl's interference is calamitous, for by compelling Dencombe to leave she causes his death. In reference to the girl's action, James speaks of "the brutality of her good conscience" (XVI, 100). Her effort to "save" Doctor Hugh, which is mainly motivated by selfishness, causes disaster. The telegraphist and Nanda Brookenham both act from laudable motives—to save others. Although the interference by the telegraphist causes no personal injury, it abets an immorality. Nanda's meddling is more culpable, for it establishes Aggie in society and gives her the liberty to corrupt herself; more important, it destroys Mitchy's life.

Fleda Vetch succeeds in saving Owen Gereth from dishonor and Mrs. Gereth from theft, but the practical result of her conscientiousness is that both are faced with a lifetime of unhappiness. But Fleda Vetch is closer in intelligence and maturity to Isabel Archer than she is to Nanda Brookenham, because Fleda's motive is to remain free herself from external influences and not to shelter others. Her interference, more negative than positive, in the affairs of the Gereths is an unavoidable result of her adherence to personal integrity. But, given the nature of society, any interference in the lives of others, regardless of motive, produces disorder and suffering. The reasons are that society itself is based on evil principles and that the innocent is unable to foresee the consequences of his action. His imperception, however, is not due entirely to the disparity between appearance and reality (for example, the disparity between Little Aggie's outward behavior and her latent nature), but also to his own serious deficiencies.

James's most ironic and most elaborate treatments of the "salvation" theme are "The Pupil," "The Turn of the Screw," and *The*

Sacred Fount. In each, evil is either unimpeded or increased by the person whose role it is to try to save others from destruction. Each of the three stories concerns an uninvolved character who finds himself in the midst of a situation in which a person or group of persons is being corrupted by another person or group of persons.

Pemberton, of "The Pupil" (1891), is the tutor of a bright and sensitive child, Morgan Moreen, whose parents are perpetually on the brink of poverty. The Moreens are social climbers who travel about Europe in an unsuccessful attempt to form attachments with rich, titled families in order to satisfy their social pretensions and arrange advantageous marriages for their older children. The main effect of their wandering is that the neglected Morgan lacks the love from his parents necessary to sustain him. The Moreens are not active agents of evil, and their malignity is negative rather than positive. But the child dies when the parents completely divorce themselves from him and ask the tutor to adopt him. The tutor himself is badly misused by the Moreens; they pay him no salary and exploit his affection for Morgan, whom they leave entirely to his care. The tutor sacrifices his own life to save the child from the influence of his parents. He provides for him materially as well as he can from his meager savings and attempts to compensate for the love denied the child by his parents. Thus the story amounts to a kind of morality tale, in which good and evil struggle for the possession of a human soul.

Pemberton, the tutor, not only sacrifices his own promising future to save Morgan, but also is an emotionally mature person whose dealings with Morgan delay the child's eventual demise. Also, unlike Mrs. Wix, the governess in *What Maisie Knew* (1897), Pemberton has no selfish reasons for remaining with Morgan; he is motivated by love only. The power of evil is stronger than the power of good in "The Pupil," but good, as represented by Pemberton, is unequivocal and valuable.

The governess in "The Turn of the Screw" (1898), however, has obvious emotional and intellectual shortcomings. Her position parallels Pemberton's. She finds herself in the midst of an unspeakable evil, for she discovers that the children she is to instruct are visited by the ghosts of two dead servants who try to gain possession of them. In "The Turn of the Screw" and *The Sacred Fount*, the outsider, whose mission it is to save the threatened innocents, faces an evil far more menacing than in "The Pupil." But the outsider himself is far less adequate. The governess differs from Pemberton in being emotionally like the telegraphist of "In the Cage." Unlike Pemberton, who accepts his position strictly as an economic matter, the governess is attracted to her job because of a foolish romantic attachment to her employer. And as the girl in the cage wishes to "do something" for Captain Everard in order to justify her existence in his world, so the governess soothes herself after her first encounter with Quint's ghost:

> . . . I was giving pleasure—if he ever thought of it!—to the person to whose pressure I had yielded. What I was doing was what he had earnestly hoped and directly asked of me, and that I *could*, after all, do it proved even a greater joy than I had expected (XII, 174).

Like the telegraphist, the governess is an easy victim of illusion. Idealizing Bly, she is enchanted by the beauty of the picturesque old country house and the surrounding landscape: ". . . I had the view of a castle of romance inhabited by a rosy sprite, such a place as would somehow, for diversion of the young idea, take all colour out of story-books and fairy tales. Wasn't it just a story-book over which I had fallen a-doze and a-dream?" (XII, 163). James develops a terrifying irony by revealing the true nature of Bly and contrasting the ugly real ghosts with the imagined garden of bliss. But the controlling irony is psychologically justified, for in the prologue to the story James characterizes the governess as immature and highly imaginative. "She was young, untried, nervous" (XII, 155), the daughter of a country minister, overly sensitive to both beauty and ugliness, and inclined to be naïve and excessively emotional in her reactions to new experience.

Like Pemberton, the governess, once exposed to the malignity of Quint and Miss Jessel, conceives of her duty as essentially moral: "The children in especial I should thus fence about and absolutely save" (XII, 195); "I was there to protect and defend the little creatures in the world the most bereaved and the most loveable, the appeal of whose helplessness had suddenly become only too explicit . . ." (XII, 199). In "The Turn of the Screw" the issues are the same as in "The Pupil," but in the former James isolates the metaphysical aspect of evil: "It was like fighting with a demon for a human soul . . ." (XII, 303). James dramatizes the struggle of good and evil in abstraction; he deals with the morality play theme in its largest dimension.

Robert B. Heilman's essay "*The Turn of the Screw* as Poem" suggests that James has stressed the disparity between the governess's moral purpose and her achieved results. Through careful analysis of imagery and diction, Heilman demonstrates that the story parallels the Fall of Man legend. The recurrent light imagery suggests "the dawn of existence"; the children suggest "the childhood of the race." Bly is described as an Eden; the movement of the seasons from June to November reflects the moral movement from innocence to fall. Quint has "the characteristics of a snake"; Miss Jessel resembles the Miltonic fallen angel. After submitting to evil, the children reveal a precocious awareness, indicative of their having eaten of the Tree of Knowledge. What seems most significant is that

> From the start the words used by the governess suggest that James is attaching to her the quality of a savior, not only in a general sense, but with certain Christian associations. She uses words like "atonement"; she speaks of herself as an "expiatory victim," of her "pure suffering," and at various times—twice in the final scene—of her "torment." [1]

Though somewhat overingenious, Heilman's interpretation of "The Turn of the Screw" is persuasive. Yet it ignores the irony that James achieves by his references to the governess as a Christlike savior. The governess, for all her devotion and agony, not only does not save the children; she also helps to damn them.

The governess shows her deficiencies in both understanding and action. For the most part, the children completely deceive her. She realizes too late that their "angelic" appearances conceal corrupted souls. Their various tricks and deceptions invariably succeed; little Miles is especially charming so that Flora can meet Miss Jessel. But it is in her behavior that the governess's weakness becomes most obvious. She is rarely other than impetuous and hysterical. Her judgment is usually mistaken and her direction of the children incompetent. Her overprotectiveness gives Miles the weapon he needs to escape her and gain free access to Quint, for he rightly insists that he is not being treated as a normal boy of his age. When the governess accuses Flora of meeting Miss Jessel by the lake, the child feigns innocence and fear of her protectress, and thereby gains the right to be taken away from her.

In the dramatic concluding scene, the governess attempts to save little Miles by eliciting a confession from him. She recognizes the difficulty of her plan:

> I could only get on at all by taking "nature" into my confidence and my account, by treating my monstrous ordeal as a push in a direction unusual, of course, and unpleasant, but demanding after all, for a fair front, only another turn of the screw of ordinary human virtue (XII, 295).

The governess has the will but not the means to save Miles. In a situation requiring supreme delicacy, she confronts the child, who wavers precariously between salvation and damnation. While Quint and the governess both strive for his soul, the child himself is in a state of utmost spiritual distress, so that only a kind of divine intervention can bring him to the side of good.

In the final scene with Miles, the governess's weakest human quality is emphasized—her self-concern. Not only is there no grace, but the human agent of good is fallible. In her pride the governess thinks not of Miles so much as of herself. After Miles confesses to stealing the letter which she has written to his uncle, the governess's first thought is not of the spiritual significance, not of the magnanimity of Miles's confession, but of "my personal triumph" (XII, 305). As the child blurts out his repentance, the governess continues to think primarily of herself, of the fact that her previous inductions were correct. "He almost smiled at me in the desolation of his surrender, which was indeed practically, by this time, so complete that I ought to have left it there. But I was infatuated—I was blind with victory . . ." (XII, 306). In her exhilaration, the governess, as she realizes, proceeds imprudently.

She questions and accuses Miles with brutality.² James makes it clear that through her indelicacy, she forces Miles to look elsewhere for support—to Quint, who is standing behind the boy on the other side of the window. When she questions the child about the crimes which caused him to be expelled from school, her enthusiasm makes her reckless:

> But the next after that I must have sounded stern enough. "What *were* these things?"
>
> My sternness was all for his judge, his executioner; yet it made him avert himself again, and that movement made *me*, with a single bound and an irrepressible cry, spring straight upon him. For there again, against the glass, as if to blight his confession and stay his answer, was the hideous author of our woe—the white face of damnation. I felt a sick swim at the drop of my victory and all the return of my battle, so that the wildness of my veritable leap only served as a great betrayal (XII, 308).

Gripped by hysteria, the governess simultaneously shelters the child and questions him, with even more anxiety and terror. When Miles asks her whom she is staring at, whether "It's *he*," the governess

> was so determined to have all my proof that I flashed into ice to challenge him. "Whom do you mean by 'he'?"
>
> "Peter Quint—you devil!" His face gave again, round the room, its convulsed supplication. "*Where?*"
>
> They are in my ears still, his supreme surrender of the name and his tribute to my devotion. "What does he matter now, my own?—what will he *ever* matter? *I* have you," I launched at the beast, "but he has lost you for ever!" Then for the demonstration of my work, "There, *there!*" I said to Miles (XII, 309).

The governess's anxiety to have her suspicions and actions justified, her solipsism, has a terrifying effect on Miles. Her excessive self-concern emerges in her determination "to have all my proof," her hasty and irreflective "Whom do you mean by 'he'?" and her stress on "his tribute to my devotion." The climax of the scene

occurs when the governess, egotistically and disastrously, points
out Quint to Miles with her "There, *there!*"—for the demonstra-
tion of her work. Thus she literally turns the child over to Quint.
In view of the governess's misdirected goodness and rashness,
Miles's "you devil" has double significance. The phrase not only
indicates, as Heilman observes, that the child has lost all moral
perception, so that in his state of damnation good is evil and evil
good,[3] but also that the governess is doing the work of the devil,
for she is certainly aiding rather than hindering Quint, and that
she is, if not a malignant force like the demons, a grotesque person
who would seem Satanic to any child. Edmund Wilson overstates
the case when he writes that "the governess has literally frightened him to death," [4] but she has so terrified him that he gives
himself over to Quint.

It is unnecessary to rely on Wilson's Freudian interpretation of
the governess's behavior, for not only are her final witless efforts
in accordance with James's characterization of her and with the
logic of the story, but also she resembles those other outsiders or
agents of good who frequent the fiction of James's middle period.
Usually characterized as emotionally and intellectually inadequate, they stand for human imperfection. They are objective
portraits of James's conception of the ineptitude and weakness of
good in a world dominated by evil. In addition, they represent a
harsher evaluation of the romantic view of life, based on illusion
rather than good sense—a view shared by James's earlier American protagonists, who do not, however, significantly cause ill to
others. Since there is no divine providence, no grace, no supernatural good, the agent of salvation is bound to fail—so much so
that he may contribute to the victory of evil.[5]

There are several links between "The Turn of the Screw" and
The Sacred Fount (1901). While in "The Pupil" and "The Turn
of the Screw" the outsider occupies an inferior social position—
as tutor and governess—and the victims of evil are in both cases
children, in *The Sacred Fount* the outsider is a gentleman spending a weekend at a country house and the victims are adults. But
the observer's relation to evil is essentially the same as in the
previous two stories. The narrator is himself uninvolved in the
malignant tangle—which in *The Sacred Fount* is sexual—but is

the only person fully aware of the meaning of the superficially tranquil activities at Newmarch.

Unlike the governess, however, the observer of *The Sacred Fount* is inactive, concerned not with restoring good but only with understanding evil. But even more than the governess, he is unpleasant, if not obnoxious. He is an egotist whose concern with the affairs of others is purely intellectual. As soon as he boards the train for Newmarch, the narrator begins to scrutinize his fellow guests. He recognizes that Grace Brissenden, whom he has known to be far older in appearance than in years, has undergone a remarkable transformation, so that she now appears unnaturally young. Correspondingly, he detects a marked alteration in Gilbert Long, who has always in the past been dull and boorish, but who now amazes the narrator with his wit and intelligence. Upon arriving at Newmarch, the narrator finds an unfortunate change in Guy Brissenden, Grace's husband, who, previously youthful in appearance, now seems an old man. The observer tries to find a logic in these three transformations and induces that Grace Brissenden is draining her husband, sapping his youth and vitality. Therefore, he reasons that for the pattern to be complete there must be a source for Long's new-found wit and, after a lengthy search, concludes that the source is May Server. In this fantasy, James objectifies his notion of the depleting power of sex.[6] But the other theme of the tale is that of the narrator, whose scientific interest in the corruption of Newmarch is, as he recognizes, "wanting in taste."[7]

As the narrator of "The Turn of the Screw" craves to prove that the horrible deeds and visions she has seen actually existed, so the narrator of *The Sacred Fount* always searches for evidence that his surmises correspond with reality. In the process of his investigation, he reflects, "I had created nothing but a clue or two to the larger comprehension I still needed, yet I positively found myself overtaken by a mild artistic glow." Carried away by his mental accomplishments, much like the governess in her final scene with Miles, the narrator is involved only with his own ingenuity: his reference to "my private triumph" echoes the governess's "my personal triumph." His egotism emerges as the narrator, dispassionately studying the morbid relationships among the other guests and realizing that his own speculations have a basis in fact, thinks, "It was the coming true that was the proof of the enchantment, which, moreover, was naturally never so great as when such coming was, to such a degree and by the most romantic stroke of all, the fruit of one's own wizardry." [8]

Though his pride of knowing is almost a pathological obsession, only through knowing can the narrator exist at Newmarch (which, like many of James's country-house settings, may be taken as a microcosm of all society). To become involved is to become either sinned-against or sinner. Knowledge, however, is a kind of action, for, just as the governess can save Miles only by eliciting a confession from him, the "I" of *The Sacred Fount* can save the predatory Mrs. Briss only by forcing her to admit her guilt. (It must be kept in mind that whereas the governess's motive is to save the children, the houseguest's is to satisfy his curiosity.) There is a striking similarity between the last scenes of the two novels. The climax of each is reached when the observer confronts the sinner with his guilt. As is always the case with James, evil is inconsistent with knowledge—the good characters are incapable of perpetrating evil because they fully understand; therefore, if Miles and Grace Brissenden would acknowledge their guilt they would be saved.

In an excellent essay on *The Sacred Fount*, R. P. Blackmur finds in the narrator a personification of the consciences of the other characters; he is, in effect, the alter ego of the social group at Newmarch. Blackmur writes that in the narrator's climactic scene with Grace Brissenden he "has given [Grace] the butter and honey of his imagination to eat, so that . . . she might know to refuse the evil, and choose the good." On the symbolic level, then, the narrator is "the projected image of conscience," [9] though on the literal level he is an overly curious snooper.

Like the governess, the all-observant guest is impersonal. He is nameless and characterless (it is not entirely clear whether he is a man or a woman). In "In the Cage" James stresses the self-destructiveness of the vicarious impersonal life. But in "The Turn of the Screw" and *The Sacred Fount* there are no counterparts of the girl's Mr. Mudge, the person with whom she may live a life of her own. The governess and the snooping guest are denied the personal life. They are faced with the dilemma either of becoming fully human by taking part in a society they know to be corrupt or of remaining aloof from life as incomplete human beings. F. O. Matthiessen suggests that the real function of such people resembles that of Tiresias,[10] doomed to know and to suffer for the sins of all, but unable to restore good. Like Eliot's Prufrock, Tiresias-like himself, James's observer may be fastidious, even ridiculous; and like the Tiresias of *The Waste Land* he may find intelligence a liability. Although extreme in his ineffectualness, the narrator of *The Sacred Fount* is nevertheless a characteristic hero of James's middle-period fiction.

THE GREAT GREY BABYLON

James's London differs obviously from the America and Europe of his earlier international fiction. Unlike Newport or Schenectady, London is tightly organized and tends to submerge the individual; unlike Paris or Rome, it has no immediate connection with the past and is devoted to modernity rather than tradition. James describes it as a society in which the old world forms are dead; there is no more concern for dignity, for honor, for politeness, for loyalty. The Bellegardes of *The American* are partly redeemed by their adherence to an ancient system. With the decline of the *noblesse*, however, expediency replaces tradition, and sheer material greed, rather than pride of name, becomes the dominant principle of a society.

In his notebooks James writes of

> the great modern collapse of all the forms and 'superstitions' and respects, good and bad, and restraints and mysteries—a vivid and mere showy general hit at the decadences and vulgarities and confusions and masculinizations and feminizations—the materializations and abdications and intrusions, and Americanizations, the lost sense, the brutalized manner —the publicity, the newspapers, the general revolution, the failure of fastidiousness.[11]

Certainly much of James's feeling stems from his own fastidiousness, his religious devotion to forms and admiration for the past.

Yet much of his social criticism in the London novels has a valid basis. For at the heart of his indictment of "the great grey Babylon" [12] of London is his revulsion from its egotism, its materialism, and its pragmatism. Manners transcend the self; they implicitly subordinate it to the larger social whole. Likewise the old manners of Europe deprecate material acquisition for its own sake and combat mere efficiency. Modern society promotes the passions of greed and lust, whereas the old world supports a nobler concept of human nature.

In his preface to "The Altar of the Dead," James refers to London as "the densest and most materialized aggregation of men upon earth, the society most wedded by all its conditions to the immediate and the finite." [13] Its passion for adultery, for money, for status are unmodified by delicacy or tact. Removed from a system of manners, such conduct represents the norm of society rather than its aberrations. Therefore, when James points out the tastelessness and the modernity of his characters he establishes their grossness of conduct as well. The vulgarization of standards in the society of *The Awkward Age* indicates moral deterioration:

> "beauty, in London . . . staring glaring obvious knock-down beauty, as plain as a poster on a wall, an advertisement of soap or whiskey, something that speaks to the crowd and crosses the footlights, fetches such a price in the market that the absence of it, for a woman with a girl to marry, inspires endless terrors and constitutes for the wretched pair (to speak of mother and daughter alone) a sort of social bankruptcy. London doesn't love the latent or the lurking, has neither time nor taste nor sense for anything less discernible than the red flag in front of the steam-roller. It wants cash over the counter and letters ten feet high" (IX, 25).

Most of James's Londoners are members of the leisure class, either of the aristocracy or of the wealthy commercial set. James was oppressed by the decline of the British nobility, the neglect of the old sense of high standards and obligations. Such country-house gatherings as those in *The Sacred Fount* and *The Awkward Age* have nothing of the easy cultured life and graceful manner of

the society of Gardencourt in *The Portrait of a Lady*. They even
lack the fierce loyalty to family and name that marks the English
gentry in "A Passionate Pilgrim" and "An International Episode."
Sir Claude has none of the dignity and stature of Lord Warburton.
James expresses his feeling toward the British upper class in a
letter:

> The condition of that body seems to me to be in many ways
> very much the same rotten and *collapsible* one as that of the
> French aristocracy before the revolution—minus cleverness
> and conversation; or perhaps it's more like the heavy, con-
> gested and depraved Roman world upon which the barbar-
> ians came down. In England the Huns and Vandals will have
> to come *up*—from the black depths of the (in the people)
> enormous misery, though I don't think the Attila is quite yet
> found—in the person of Mr. Hyndman. At all events, much
> of English life is grossly materialistic and wants blood-
> letting.[14]

Most often James exposes London society from the point of view
of the individual Londoner surrounded on all sides by either
sordidness or meaninglessness. His children are all more or less
"in the cage," estranged in the midst of "a society in which for
the most part people [are] occupied only with chatter . . ."
(XI, 6). His decayed old men like George Stransom and Mr.
Longdon embody an older period of history in which values
dictated behavior and meaning stood behind appearances. To
James modern civilization is a threat to the self. Not only is the
sanctity of the individual person jeopardized by the decline of
refinement and subtlety and the rise of the crass vehicles of public
communication, but the mechanical nature of society—cold,
harsh, and efficient—threatens to defeat the precious human
elements. Thus, for James, the replacing of the formal letter by
the informal note symbolizes London at the end of the nineteenth
century:

> Good manners are a succession of details, and I don't mean
> to say that she [London] doesn't attend to them when she
> has time. She has it, however, but seldom—*que voulez-vous?*

Perhaps the matter of note-writing is as good an example as
another of what certain of the elder traditions inevitably
have become in her hands. She lives by notes—they are her
very heart-beats; but those that bear her signature are as
disjointed as the ravings of delirium, and have nothing but a
postage stamp in common with the epistolary art.[15]

Condensation and efficiency, for James, are incompatible with the
human and the meaningful. They necessitate the elimination of
the intelligent and the sensitive approaches to life; they deprive
human intercourse of the finer intellectual basis that gives it value.

In a notebook entry James records the *donnée* of a possible
story:

Yesterday at the Borthwicks', at Hampstead, something
that Lady Tweedmouth said about the insane frenzy of futile
occupation imposed by the London season, added itself to
the hideous realization in my own mind—recently so deepened—to suggest that a 'subject' may very well reside in
some picture of this overwhelming, self-defeating chaos or
cataclysm toward which the whole thing is drifting. The picture residing, exemplified, in the experience of some tremendously exposed and intensely conscious individual—the
deluge of people, the insane movement for movement, the
ruin of thought, of life, the negation of work, of literature,
the swelling, roaring crowds, the 'where are you going?,' the
age of Mrs. Jack, the figure of Mrs. Jack, the American, the
nightmare—the individual consciousness—the mad, ghastly
climax or denouement. It's a splendid subject—if worked
round a personal action—situation.[16]

This passage, written in 1895, might well serve as the "germ" for
all of James's London fiction. It is a striking observation, close to
much of recent literature in its sense of the present, in its perception of the sickness of modern society. The world of pointless
movement in Eliot's "The Hollow Men" parallels the London
world James describes. This passage also shows that James's point
of view is outward from the sensitive person. The world is evil
insofar as it causes suffering. In itself thoroughly dehumanized, it

can corrupt only the superior person, whose values are on a higher plane—the human rather than the commercial or the animal. James's sensitive London characters all live "under the awful doom of general dishumanization." [17]

What James finds to be inhuman about London is its neglect of the simple yet important matters of living: such essential human relationships as those between husband and wife, parent and child, and living and dead are perverted or destroyed. The basis of "The Pupil," *What Maisie Knew,* and *The Awkward Age* is the subordination of family responsibility to greed or lust. As Sir Claude says in *What Maisie Knew,* "there *are* no family women —hanged if there are! None of them want any children—hanged if they do!" (XI, 61). *The Spoils of Poynton* concerns an antagonism between mother and son. *The Awkward Age* deals with the corruption of marriage. *The Sacred Fount, What Maisie Knew,* and "The Turn of the Screw" also treat varying perversions of love. As normal human intercourse is reduced to the telegraphed communication in "In the Cage," so parental and marital relationships are settled in the law courts in *The Spoils of Poynton* and *What Maisie Knew.*

In James's middle period the blackness of the past is replaced by the grossness of the present. Thus the divorce court, rather than the ancestral manor, is the symbol of a corrupt society. The social acceptability of divorce represents for James the decline of marriage. Though both Gilbert Osmond and Urbain de Bellegarde pervert marriage out of egotism, they nevertheless recognize its inviolability and sanctity. From *What Maisie Knew,* as well as "A London Life," it is apparent that James finds little difference between adultery and divorce: both are equally grave violations of the marriage vow. Sexual relations dominate James's London fiction in a peculiarly lurid way. The symmetrical compounding of matches in *What Maisie Knew,* the welter of cryptic telegrams between the lovers in "In the Cage," perversion and the suggestion of homosexuality in "The Turn of the Screw," [18] and the intrinsic horror of sex in *The Sacred Fount*—all point to James's habit of identifying sex per se with the ugly and the unnatural.

Usually, however, James links physical passion with divorce

and adultery, which, in his essential conservatism, he considers
serious wrongs. Sexual relations are more often indirectly than
directly evil, since they disrupt marriage and lead to the dereliction of responsibility. The gravity of the sexual offense is more
apparent in its disastrous effect on the outsider to the relationship
—usually the innocent child—than, as in *The Sacred Fount,* on
the participant.

In those London stories in which divorce and adultery do not
provide the sordid background—most prominently in *The Spoils
of Poynton*—the sin is greed for material possessions. In his
preface to *The Spoils* James writes:

> One thing was . . . in the sordid situation, on the first blush,
> and one thing only . . . the sharp light it might project on
> that most modern of our current passions, the fierce appetite
> for the upholsterer's and joiner's and brazier's work, the
> chairs and tables, the cabinets and presses, the material odds
> and ends, of the more labouring ages.[19]

In themselves, of course, the "things" are neither good nor evil.
Yet the possession of them and the means by which one gains
possession of them may be evil. Only Fleda Vetch holds moral
principles over acquisition: both Mona Brigstock and Mrs. Gereth
injure others to gain the spoils.

Whether one is devoted to sexual lust or material greed, his
egotism has the effect of crippling the life of another, usually
an innocent child deserted by his parents. The theme of the
dereliction of parental duty is inseparable from the theme of lust
and greed in *What Maisie Knew,* "The Pupil," and *The Awkward Age.* The children in these stories need love to survive, but
their elders subordinate responsibility to passion. The other notable children of James's London fiction are also neglected: Miles
and Flora of "The Turn of the Screw" are orphaned children,
wards of an uncle who never sees them, placed in the care of an
obtuse maid and a hysterical governess.

In the London stories there are no single villains; society itself
is the villain. In the world of *The Portrait of a Lady,* Mme. Merle
and Henrietta Stackpole as well as Gilbert Osmond and Lord

Warburton can exist and prosper as independent persons. The social situation is fluid and spacious enough to contain a multitude of different types. Paradoxically, in James's London, in which the manners which have upheld the older society are dead, a higher consistency is demanded on the part of the characters. The social structure of *The Awkward Age* is far more rigid than that of any continental group. Adherence to the ways of modern life restricts individual freedom more than adherence to the ways of the aristocracy.

Therefore the dominant figures of London society are merely typical. Such characters as Sir Claude and Mrs. Brookenham represent the whole tone of a society. They have no independent selves; removed from their environments they are nothing. Society is an artificial form of existence, for it makes no provision for the personal element. As Scott Homer of "Mrs. Medwin" says, in reference to those who live in and for society, "They're dead" (XVIII, 491); they can exist only as social creatures and not at all as persons.

For this reason the symmetrical pattern of divorces and re-matches in *What Maisie Knew* indicates more than James's concern for structural balance. Rather the ludicrous regularity with which Maisie's parents pair off establishes the sameness of their lives. In *The Awkward Age* the stylized conversation cramps the individual. Vanderbank and Mitchy stand slightly aloof from the immorality of Mrs. Brook's group, but Petherton, Lady Fanny, the Duchess, Tishy Grendon, and Mrs. Brook herself differ only in the accidental matters of appearance, intelligence, and economic status.

In such a society the individual who is not absorbed by the group is either excluded or preyed upon. Sir Claude must finally decide whether to adhere to his weak moral sense and to his liking for Maisie or to his illicit attachment to Mrs. Beale. His decision is between self and society: to reject Mrs. Beale for Maisie would be equivalent to isolating himself from an environment which recognizes adultery as normal. Drawn into her mother's group, Nanda must retreat with Mr. Longdon to preserve her independence of thought and judgment. In short, as

James puts it (with considerable understatement), London society is one in which "individual appreciations of propriety have
not been formally allowed for." [20]

London society of the 1890's lacks the obvious sinister quality
of the Europe which ensnared Newman and Isabel. There are no
ancestral curses, no gloomy chateaux, no mysteries, no Gothic
overtones. No superificial veneer disguises the precise nature of
the vain and avaricious Londoners. Appearance and reality correspond in such characters as Mrs. Brook and Beale Farange.
Here, for example, is James's description of Maisie's mother:

> The sole flaw in Ida's beauty was a length and reach of arm
> conducive perhaps to her having so often beaten her ex-
> husband at billiards, a game in which she showed a superior-
> ity largely accountable, as she maintained, for the resentment
> finding expression in his physical violence. Billiards was her
> great accomplishment and the distinction her name always
> first produced the mention of. Notwithstanding some very
> long lines everything about her that might have been large
> and that in many women profited by the licence was, with a
> single exception, admired and cited for its smallness. The
> exception was her eyes, which might have been of mere
> regulation size, but which overstepped the modesty of na-
> ture; her mouth, on the other hand, was barely perceptible,
> and odds were freely taken as to the measurement of her
> waist. She was a person who, when she was out—and she was
> always out—produced everywhere a sense of having been
> seen often, the sense indeed of a kind of abuse of visibility,
> so that it would have been, in the usual places, rather vulgar
> to wonder at her (XI, 7–8).

This description approaches caricature. Certainly Ida lacks both
the superficial attraction of an Osmond and the portentousness of
an Urbain de Bellegarde. Ida is blatantly ludicrous in both appearance and behavior.

The prevading tone of *What Maisie Knew*, like that of *The
Spoils of Poynton* and *The Awkward Age*, is that of light comedy
of manners. But James does not lessen the gravity of the transgres-

sions of his comic characters. *The Awkward Age* has all the glitter and brilliance of dialogue of a Wilde comedy, plus the light approach toward marriage. Were it not for the presence of the innocent (Nanda), the tone of the society would set the tone of the novel. But the innocent requires that the entire proceedings be judged on moral grounds. Actually, to James, the presence of a superior person and the effect of the frivolous group on the person give the society meaning. In his preface to *Maisie* James remarks that without Maisie the other characters would have no interest:

> They become, as she deals with them, the stuff of poetry and tragedy and art; she has simply to wonder, as I say, about them, and they begin to have meanings, aspects, solidities, connexions—connexions with the "universal!"—that they could scarce have hoped for. Ida Farange alone, so to speak, or Beale alone, that is either of them otherwise connected—what intensity, what "objectivity" (the most developed degree of *being* anyhow thinkable for them) would they have? How would they repay at all the favour of our attention? [21]

Through the agency of Maisie, James shows the objectively comic to be subjectively tragic and the superficially pleasant to be essentially evil. Quentin Anderson points out that one of James's fictional methods is to convert the reader, to change his attitude toward the subject matter. [22] Maisie's presence transforms social comedy into personal tragedy, as the light approach to marriage by the adults is demonstrated to be inadequate.

But if the Londoners are comic they are also—and obviously—unimportant. They lack the stature of the early villains, just as their deeds are sins of the weak rather than sins of the strong. Like Isabel Archer and Euphemia Cleve, the telegraphist and Maisie are betrayed by illusion, each finding a glamorous superiority in a man who is little more than a pompous and stupid fop. To find value in the appearance of Captain Everard and Sir Claude—men whom Isabel Archer would easily see through—requires an extreme naïveté, a quality which James stresses in his child victims. The easily duped victims are far more vulnerable than their

American predecessors precisely because of their naïveté. They
are readily taken advantage of without the assistance of elaborate
intrigue or calculation by the adults. It is unnecessary for Maisie's
parents to deceive her as Osmond deceives Isabel. Because appearance and reality correspond, the innocent must be given the
simplicity and credulity of a child.

Since society bears no sinister appearance, James employs scene
to suggest its deviation from a norm. In his British fiction nature
plays a major role in establishing moral tone. The pastoral settings
of country-house activity ironically contrast with the sordidness
of the characters. The observer frequently becomes entranced by
the surrounding beauty of a social gathering, so that his apprehen-
sion of what the scene conceals comes as a shock. In his early
American stories James uses the placid and harmonious countryside to symbolize the quiet, graceful lives of such families as the
Wentworths. He uses scene for the opposite purpose in *The
Awkward Age*. A rented country house seems to suggest a
relaxed and eminently humane social entity:

> The lower windows of the great white house, which stood
> high and square, opened to a wide flagged terrace, the parapet
> of which, an old balustrade of stone, was broken in the
> middle of its course by a flight of stone steps that descended
> to a wonderful garden. The terrace had the afternoon shade
> and fairly hung over the prospect that dropped away and
> circled it—the prospect, beyond the series of gardens, of
> scattered splendid trees and green glades, an horizon mainly
> of woods. . . . The scene had an expectant stillness that
> [Nanda] was too charmed to desire to break; she watched it,
> listened to it, followed with her eyes the white butterflies
> among the flowers below her, then gave a start as the cry of a
> peacock came to her from an unseen alley (IX, 203).

What begins to take on the appearance of a Garden of Eden
soon becomes a kind of Garden of Gethsemane; [23] Nanda meets
the nervous, patronizing Vanderbank and realizes that he will
neglect her and leave her to struggle for her own existence in her
mother's circle.

In *The Sacred Fount* the description of nature surrounding

Newmarch emphasizes an unnatural calmness and stillness. Here, as Elisabeth Luther Cary has observed, "the tortured real is corrected by the calm ideal, and abstract synthetised beauty hangs like a brooding angel over the tangled human spectacle." [24] Yet nature not only provides a sharp contrast with the frenzied human activity, but also it suggests, through its own frozenness, the grimness of the world it surrounds:

> There was a general shade in all the lower reaches—a fine clear dusk in garden and grove, a thin suffusion of twilight out of which the greater things, the high tree-tops and pinnacles, the long crests of motionless wood and chimnied roof, rose into golden air. The last calls of birds sounded extraordinarily loud; they were like the timed, serious splashes, in wide, still water, of divers not expecting to rise again. [25]

The startling concluding metaphor, and those like it which now begin to appear frequently in James's work, suggest, as F. W. Dupee writes, "the realm of the physical and the elemental, of latent horror, of 'the thing hideously behind'." [26] Clearly James is using scene for purposes radically different from those in his earlier work. Instead of relying on conventional Gothic or pastoral settings, he creates a world in which objects of nature correspond to states of mind.

More than ever before, James in his London fiction uses the personal vision of things to convey significance. Thus meaning cannot always be clearly stated in rational terms, because it is inseparable from the emotion of the witness. The horror of the governess, the frenzied intellectualism of the weekend guest, the morbid anguish of Stransom: such feelings convey the inner corruption of James's Londoners.

Physical passion exists only in the background of James's fiction, but its moral significance is explored fully in the foreground. There is not so much as a kiss or a suggestive glance in *The Sacred Fount*, James's one novel whose major theme is physical love, but there is no escaping the full horror of sexual relations. From a glance at Mrs. Server, the victim of Gilbert Long's predatory love, the narrator grasps the quality of that love:

I saw as I had never seen before what consuming passion can make of the marked mortal on whom, with fixed beak and claws, it has settled as on a prey. She reminded me of a sponge wrung dry and with fine pores agape. Voided and scraped of everything, her shell was merely crushable.[27]

With surrealistic effect, mental images replace concrete delineation. The avoidance of graphic description of physical passion is more than compensated for by the concreteness of the images which convey its ravaging effects.

There are four major character types in James's middle-period fiction: the victimized innocent, the weak man, the fool, and the clever woman. Each in his own way has a large capacity for evil. The innocents are too rarely intelligent and thus injure through ignorance. The men are most often dependent, indecisive creatures, who prefer to ignore crises rather than face them. Owen Gereth has a kind of boyish tenderness; Sir Claude and Vanderbank have an obvious but unalloyed charm; some others, like Edward Brookenham, are so negative as to seem completely innocuous. Yet, in their retreat from all positive action, these men implicitly commit themselves to the decisions of the women who govern their lives; by default they contribute to the moral ugliness of society. The fools, on the other hand—invariably women —are violently aggressive. James writes that "the fixed constituents of almost any reproducible action are the fools who minister, at a particular crisis, to the intensity of the free spirit engaged with them." [28] Among the fools is the philistine, the woman who, through stupidity or crassness, kills the artist. A major example is Mona Brigstock, a massive force, concerned only with the grossest of material possessions. In a world largely controlled by fools, there are also the more dangerous, because more intelligent, women, who manipulate weak and foolish alike, and exploit the sensitive. None of James's stories contains a full-scale portrait of a fool, but many have as central characters those women of great exterior attraction who combine will and social (but not moral) intelligence to achieve worldly success.

Just as the evil of the fools is somewhat disguised by their absurdity, the evil of the clever women is so fused with their personal charm and social grace as to be concealed. Furthermore, these women command admiration for their remoteness from the shallowness and tastelessness of the worlds they inhabit. Even the murderess in *The Other House*, Rose Armiger, can hardly be termed a complete villainess.[29] But, though her evil is not un-mixed, it is obvious. Mrs. Gereth and Mrs. Brookenham, however, though just as willful as Rose, and ultimately as predatory, are far more ambiguous characterizations.

Both are intelligent and delightful, mistresses of society, and expert manipulators of people. Mrs. Gereth's refined love of *objets d'art* reflects taste and sensibility, in themselves admirable traits. In manner she is genuine and gracious, capable of respect and friendship for Fleda Vetch. She gains sympathy because of the repulsiveness of her antagonists: the insensitive Mona Brig-stock, who strives to possess the objects Mrs. Gereth has spent a lifetime collecting, and the brutal, unflinching injustice of the British law, which provides that the "things" rightfully belong to Mona. But when Mrs. Gereth takes the offensive she violates the Jamesian ethical code: she attempts to have Fleda gain Owen's love and win him over from Mona, thereby disregarding her son's pledge and exploiting Fleda. Thus, in spite of Mrs. Gereth's praiseworthy ambitions and sympathetic situation, she is, as James states in his notebooks, blinded to moral reality by her aggressive-ness: "*She sets the girl on him*—cynically, almost, or indecently (making her feel AGAIN how little account—in the way of fine respect—she makes of her. Touch *that*, Mrs. G.'s unconscious brutality and immorality, briefly and finely). She presses Fleda— yes—upon him . . . ."[30]

In *The Spoils of Poynton* the unethical is natural and the ethical unnatural. Mona instinctively snatches at the spoils; Owen is willing to break his pledge; Mrs. Gereth is unaware of the moral limitations of her intrigue; even Fleda is tempted to follow Mrs. Gereth's lead and seek happiness before honor. When Fleda renounces happiness, she seems perverse; she goes counter to human nature. The inclination to evil is part of human nature; guilt is universal.

The ultimate spiritual implication of *The Spoils of Poynton*
and most of James's London fiction becomes the theme of "The
Turn of the Screw." The main irony of "The Turn of the Screw"
is the disparity between the reality and the appearance of the
children. Described as angelic, even divine, in their beauty, the
children are not innocent, as they seem, but corrupted. The story
does not show, as Robert B. Heilman suggests, good becoming
evil and youth becoming age, but evil existing under the appearance of good. Charles G. Hoffmann writes that "in *The Turn of
the Screw* innocence and evil coexist as evil-in-good." But the
good is mere illusion. The children themselves consciously appear
most innocent at the very moments when they are in communication with the demons. As Oliver Evans comments, "the 'rose
flush of innocence' is never so intense as when [Miles] is most
actively engaged in positive evil." In other words, "the lambs are
not lambs at all, but tigers; the children are not really children,
but, as Mrs. Grose perceives in the end, as old as evil itself." [31]

The ultimate theme of "The Turn of the Screw" is Original
Sin. The governess speaks of the children as "blameless and
foredoomed" (XII, 217). They are blameless because foredoomed; that is, the children are evil—or inclined to evil—because of a kind of natural depravity. With all of James's characters
evil is either active or latent. For all except those of "the finer
grain" it dictates the natural course of activity. The others must
make extreme effort to remain free from complicity. Personal
evil can be avoided only by a retreat from the world—the ultimate
course for Maisie and Nanda. If one—like Fleda Vetch—is to act
for good it follows that he must seem perverse, for such conduct
is not only abnormal, but literally unnatural. In the society of a
fallen world innocence cannot survive.

"The Turn of the Screw" concerns a pair of children plagued
from infancy by evil, which they willingly accept when they
first understand its meaning. In his other stories about children,
James also treats "the death of . . . childhood." [32] Like Miles and
Flora, Maisie and Nanda are exposed to contaminating influences.
Their stories deal with the period in their lives when they acquire
knowledge. What Maisie finally knows is that her elders are
corrupt and that to remain uncorrupted herself she must reject

them. But Maisie always possesses the capacity to damn herself, as does Nanda, for whom her mother's circle, with its adulteries, intrigues, and treacheries, presents a constant temptation. The latent power for evil emerges in Little Aggie when she ceases to be a child. Even with the free spirits there is often a pride which modifies the purity of the moral sense. Fleda Vetch, the governess, and the telegraphist cannot divorce self-interest from right conduct.

In James's world of "blameless and foredoomed" people, it is not surprising to find a number who are basically honorable—who do not injure others—yet so limited as to be in part evil. In his middle period James catalogues a number of characters guilty of pride, not the gross egotism of an Osmond or even the unconscious egotism of a Mrs. Gereth, but the less offensive vanity that has the effect of blighting the self.

In a notebook entry James makes a distinction between "the pride that can harden and stiffen its heart . . . and the pride that suffers." [33] The former is the pride of John Marcher of "The Beast in the Jungle" (1903), whose excessive self-concern prohibits him from loving May Bartram; the latter is the pride of Fleda Vetch, whose loyalty to principles prevents her happiness. But Fleda does not allow her heart to harden; she would become callous and insensitive only by rejecting her higher values and pursuing mere pleasure. Many characters like Marcher enter the stories of James's middle period. George Stransom's exclusion of his betrayer, Acton Hague, causes his devotion to the dead to be imperfect. Not until he forgives Hague is Stransom's altar of the dead complete, for he still shares in the self-destroying egotism of the world he rejects. Vanderbank, of *The Awkward Age*, however, becomes increasingly hardened by a pride that leads him to find too many faults in the woman he loves. The brief "Broken Wings" (1900) is a light treatment of the theme of pride. Two lovers do not see each other for ten years because each is ashamed of his failure in his chosen career and believes the other to be successful. Meeting by accident, they realize that both have experienced the same misfortune. "What had come out . . . was that each, ten years before, had miserably misunderstood and then had turned for relief from pain to a perversity of pride" (XVI, 158). When they realize the destructiveness of their attitudes, they reunite and plan to marry, "with a final abandonment of pride that was like changing at the end of a dreadful day from tight shoes to loose ones" (XVI, 161). This is not the large and dynamic pride of Isabel Archer, through which she believes that all the world exists for her, but a narrowing rather than an expansive pride, a weakness of spirit that excludes and limits.

Just as Stransom and the couple in "Broken Wings" are essentially moral in spite of their limitations, there are other characters whose selfishness does not outweigh their goodness. Mrs. Wix, Maisie's governess, gains by contrast with Maisie's elders, but it is clear that, to emphasize Maisie's isolation, James qualifies Mrs. Wix's goodness by pointing out that her devotion to Maisie is far from selfless. Her passion for Sir Claude is ridiculous only to others; to herself the relationship with Maisie is a means of meeting and possibly winning him. Also, Mrs. Wix is desperately poor, too incompetent to be assured of regular work. To her, caring for Maisie means, among other things, steady employment. When she considers that Maisie may become the sole property of Mrs. Beale and Sir Claude, her concern is not for the welfare of the child, but for herself: "They'll take you, they'll take you, and what in the world will then become of me?" (XI, 118).

Mrs. Wix shares in the universal sin of selfhood. And with the rest of James's Londoners she inhabits a fallen world, where evil is normal and good perverse, where total good is a fiction, where the sensitive moral person cannot exist.

THE AWKWARD AGE

The Awkward Age (1899) is a study of a social situation: an awkward period during which a young single girl is exposed to the advanced conversation of her elders. According to the rules of the society, she must marry as soon as possible, before she loses her innocence of mind and thus becomes unattractive to prospective suitors. James constructs around this central theme a number of secondary issues along with a full set of characters, in order to amplify the basic *donnée*. From the situation of the girl's awkward age, the nature of a society is revealed through its relation to the situation, which in turn is given meaning because of its connection with the larger whole. The problem of the daughter, Nanda, is also her mother's; and the field of operations is Mrs. Brookenham's circle. James achieves complexity and depth through full characterization of the circle, which is a microcosm of the London world, with its indecencies, indelicacies, betrayals, intrigues, pettiness, and ugliness. Marriage, the major concern of Nanda and her mother, is, as in *The Portrait of a Lady*, also the dominant interest of the other characters: to Mrs. Brook and the Duchess, marriage is a matter of political intrigue; to the shadowy figures in the background of the novel—Cashmore, Petherton, Lady Fanny, and Mrs. Donner—it is a matter of frivolity; to Vanderbank, it is a matter of self-effacement; to Mr. Longdon, who represents the mores of a previous age, it is a matter of sacred trust and devotion.

As in *The Sacred Fount* and *What Maisie Knew*, we are never allowed to overlook the immorality of the society, because of the constant suggestion of irregular sexual behavior. Three adulteries unmistakably establish the tone of the society: Cashmore has an affair with Mrs. Donner; his wife, Lady Fanny, is about to leave for Italy with a Captain Dent-Douglas; and Lady Fanny's brother, Lord Petherton, is the Duchess's lover. This tangled web of marital and extramarital relationships exists within an even tighter circle than in *What Maisie Knew;* and, as in the earlier novel, though with less symmetry, there is also the pairing off and rematching. Petherton neglects the Duchess and takes up with her niece, Little Aggie; Lady Fanny decides not to leave with Dent-Douglas because of her attraction for Mrs. Brookenham's son, Harold; and Cashmore makes an unsuccessful bid for Nanda's favor.

While sexual promiscuity pervades the background of Mrs. Brook's circle, the foreground is dominated by the equally immoral, though less sordid, activity of the major characters. Too poor to operate with ease in her society, Mrs. Brook is forced to plot to gain a fortune. Thus, like Mrs. Gereth of *The Spoils of Poynton*, she exploits others in order to insure her own material comfort. Though Nanda loves Vanderbank, her mother promotes her marriage to Mitchy, for not only is Van poor and Mitchy wealthy but Mrs. Brook wants Van, a key figure in her circle, for herself. The novel chronicles Mrs. Brook's numerous maneuvers to acquire a large income and keep Van, all the while neglecting the interests and desires of Nanda. But the monetary theme enters the novel in other ways as well. Harold Brookenham, one of James's children who do not preserve innocence, has the function of revealing his mother's true nature, for he has her ambitions and unscrupulousness, unredeemed by her wit and grace. Harold continually and systematically takes money from his mother's friends and parasitically invites himself—at his mother's urging—to other people's houses. Petherton bleeds Mitchy of his wealth; Vanderbank is sorely tempted to marry Nanda for money.

To James's mind unrestrained commercialism indicates the depravity of a culture. In *The Awkward Age* the decline of manners is in inverse ratio to the increased association of human institutions with money. Thus Mr. Longdon, who represents the moral norm of the novel,[34] is shocked when he learns that Mitchy has rented a country house:

> "Now this sudden invasion of somebody's—heaven knows whose—house, and our dropping down on it like a swarm of locusts: I dare say it isn't civil to criticise it when one's going too, so almost culpably, with the stream; but what are people made of that they consent, just for money, to the violation of their homes?"
>
> Nanda wondered. . . . "But haven't people in England always let their places?"
>
> "If we're a nation of shopkeepers, you mean, it can't date, on the scale on which we show it, only from last week? No doubt, no doubt, and the more one thinks of it the more one seems to see that society—for we're *in* society, aren't we, and that's our horizon?—can never have been anything but increasingly vulgar. The point is that in the twilight of time—and I belong, you see, to the twilight—it had been made out much less how vulgar it *could* be" (IX, 219–220).

Manners are an indication of morals in *The Awkward Age*. The tastelessness of the furnishings in Tishy Grendon's parlor prepares us for the immoral behavior which occurs there. Most of the overt activity of Mrs. Brook's circle is bad-mannered. In his preface James notes that the custom of allowing the innocent daughter to participate in adult conversation is a vulgarity— "as far as possible removed even, no doubt, in its appealing 'modernity,' from that of supposedly privileged scenes of conversation twenty years ago." [35] The conversation recognizes no limits imposed by good taste; rather it delights in analyzing the illicit behavior of others, in promoting scandals, in destroying character. In his fastidiousness James—through Mr. Longdon— calls attention to the modern practice of lying about one's daughter's age to better her chances for marriage; and the crisis of the novel has as its basis the revelation that Nanda has read a French novel.

Yet *The Awkward Age* does more than condemn modern vulgarity, for behind the bad manners there is generally gross conduct. The society of *The Awkward Age* sacrifices the meaningful to the artificial, and in order to be urbane it destroys the humane. Not only is marriage made a business and a game and the child a victim of the parent's opportunism rather than a recipient of his love, but friendship, loyalty, and sincerity are replaced by betrayal and hypocrisy, or else they become so superficial as to amount to their opposites. Mrs. Brook's group is bound by a joint interest in good talk, which is good precisely because of its ironies and innuendoes, its callousness to privacy, its wit at the expense of others' foibles. At one point the Duchess remarks, "What are parties given in London for but that enemies may meet?" (IX, 103). Mr. Longdon's observation would be considered by the insider as irrelevant, but it strikes at the heart of both the merits and weaknesses of the circle: after Vanderbank casually remarks, "What's London life after all? It's tit for tat," Mr. Longdon replies, "Ah but what becomes of friendship?" (IX, 20). Vanderbank, who recognizes the inadequacy of Mrs. Brook's circle, but—like Prufrock—is too weak and dependent to withdraw from it, later crystalizes Mr. Longdon's objection: "What you mean at any rate . . . is that we're cold and sarcastic and cynical, without the soft human spot" (IX, 34). As her group overlooks the province of the heart in human intercourse, so Mrs. Brook is coldly rational in promoting Nanda's marriage.

Closely allied to the absence of friendship is the absence of

loyalty. Mr. Longdon's priestlike loyalty to the dead Lady Julia
serves as an instructive contrast to the betrayals that characterize
Mrs. Brook's coterie. Vanderbank betrays Mr. Longdon's trust
and Nanda's chances for happiness by refusing to marry her out
of pride and squeamishness. Mr. Longdon is loyal to the memory
of Lady Julia: he shelters her granddaughter from her environment, while Vanderbank vainly decides that Nanda is beyond
possible salvation. In order to embarrass Van and keep him from
marrying Nanda, Mrs. Brook betrays his confidence; she informs
Mitchy of Mr. Longdon's proposal to give Nanda a fortune if
Van will marry her. Mitchy is betrayed by Little Aggie, who is
unfaithful to him immediately after their marriage. Most important, Mrs. Brook betrays Nanda: she humiliates her before Mr.
Longdon and the entire circle. On the other hand, the finer
characters—those removed from or on the periphery of the circle
—act from nobility and loyalty. In her own curious way Nanda
is loyal to Mitchy when she takes responsiblity for his hapless
marriage, which he originally agrees to out of loyalty to Nanda.
Finally, Nanda, with Mitchy's aid, reveals a loyalty to the very
people who betray her: she urges Van and Mitchy not to desert
her mother; she urges Mr. Longdon to forgive Van. Mitchy and
Mr. Longdon together agree to provide Van with money so that
he will not have lost by not marrying Nanda.

Sincerity and honesty in human dealings are replaced by
deception and indirection. The series of intrigues and counter-
intrigues depends on clandestine maneuvering and false appearances. Sincerity becomes perverted when Mrs. Brook hypocriti-
cally justifies her exposure as an act of sincerity: "If the principal
beauty of our effort to live together is . . . in our sincerity, I
simply obeyed the impulse to do the sincere thing. If we're not
sincere we're nothing" (IX, 302). The episode resembles the
scene in *The Golden Bowl* in which the Prince and Charlotte,
while speaking of their sacred duty to be faithful to their *sposi*,
embrace and begin their illicit relationship. Mitchy, Van, and
Mrs. Brook all know that the latter's manner is totally insincere,
for it is her method of keeping Van from marrying Nanda; the
conversation disguises the real nature of the incident. Thus the
three carry the scene to its conclusion, and their emphasis on the

importance of simplicity and sincerity is in complete contrast
with their actual feelings and motives. Mitchy is obviously embarrassed by Mrs. Brook's audacity; Van feels exposed and defeated; and Mrs. Brook herself is uneasy after her blow. The
episode stresses the false camaraderie of the group and the perversion of honesty. Mrs. Brook's final attempt to restore tranquility
strikes a particularly false note:

> "The thing is, don't you think?"—she appealed to Mitchy—
> "for us not to be so awfully clever as to make it believed that
> we can never be simple. We mustn't see *too* tremendous
> things—even in each other." She quite lost patience with the
> danger she glanced at. "We *can* be simple!" (IX, 303).

After this proclamation, feeling that the smoke has been cleared
and her frankness justified, Mrs. Brook proceeds to annihilate
Van and further her plans for Nanda by callously referring to
her own attachment to Van and to Van's feelings about Nanda.

Mrs. Brook's set is "past saving" (p. 20) because of its talk,
however, rather than its behavior. Although she ironically defeats
her own purposes, Mrs. Brook is motivated by her desire to hold
her school of wits together. Thus the problem of the "awkward
age" is hers more than Nanda's, for, with Nanda downstairs, she
is faced with the (to her) disastrous necessity of reducing the
high level of talk in order to keep Nanda sheltered. She chooses
to compromise Nanda rather than compromise her conversational
standards. To preserve her own circle Mrs. Brook must keep Van
and she must have money: thus she sacrifices Nanda. ". . . I
often feel as if I were a circus-woman, in pink tights and no
particular skirts, riding half a dozen horses at once" (IX, 188),
Mrs. Brook says, and without her circus she cannot exist. Mrs.
Brook, in a sense, reduces life to a kind of art. She values life as a
source of intellectual enjoyment, and, if need be, will injure
others in order to preserve her circle.

Mrs. Brook's dealings with Cashmore and his wife, Lady Fanny,
well illustrate her total devotion to wit. Early in the novel Cashmore complains to her that Lady Fanny has been accepting gifts
from unknown donors. Mrs. Brook, who, as she explains, has "a
kind of vision of things, of the wretched miseries in which you

all knot yourselves up . . ." (IX, 164–165), shrewdly analyzes
Cashmore's marital difficulties. She contends that Lady Fanny is
a magnificent pagan who acts entirely on instinct; she is thus not
to be judged on standard moral grounds. Cashmore, however, as
Mrs. Brook observes, must rationalize his own profligacy: he feels
justified in his affair with Carrie Donner only as long as he believes
his wife to be equally unfaithful. But Mrs. Brook will not give him
the support he wants, for she does not condemn Fanny. Thus she
keeps the situation in balance; things remain unresolved and
indefinite.

Mrs. Brook's intention has not been to soothe Cashmore, to
prevent scandal, or to promote a moral code, but to ensure the
continuation of what she and her circle find intellectually exciting.
Her moral neutrality, rather her total freedom from what she
would probably consider "vulgar" personal concerns, allows her
to encourage her son Harold to pursue Lady Fanny, and Cashmore to pursue Nanda, so that the tension might continue and
Lady Fanny might be prevented from leaving.

In contrast, the Duchess, who is a seeress and a moderator on a
lesser scale, has motives which are personal and opportunistic;
and Mr. Longdon, more remote but equally formidable as a kind
of stage manager, is prompted by his chivalric love for Nanda and
respect for Vanderbank. In this network of intrigues, both Mrs.
Brook and Mr. Longdon demonstrate the inadequacy of the
Duchess's motives and methods of interference. Mrs. Brook's and
Mr. Longdon's intentions, however, are mutually critical, for if
the former lack love, the latter lack art, but ultimately Mr.
Longdon's moral bias is shown to take precedence over Mrs.
Brook's intellectual bias.

The talk is objectionable not simply because it is too free, but
because it is abstracted from life. In the typical James novel, as
Jacques Barzun has pointed out, dialogue is both dramatic and
emotional; it is a substitute for physical action and is full of passion and feeling.[36] With the sophisticated intellectual chatter of
The Awkward Age, however, talk exists almost in a vacuum. In
his final scene with Nanda, Vanderbank, second only to Mrs.
Brook as a master of wit and conversation, is speechless in a genuinely human situation. His constant shaking of his foot and inane

banter reveal his incapacity to be other than superficial. As we
have seen, in the episode in which Mrs. Brook tells Mitchy of
Mr. Longdon's proposal to Van, the talk is divorced from the
actual feelings and thoughts of the characters. Mrs. Brook once
remarks, "And yet to think that after all it has been mere *talk!*"
Vanderbank replies, "Mere, mere, mere. But perhaps it's exactly
the 'mere' that has made us range so wide." And Mrs. Brook an-
swers, "You mean that we haven't had the excuse of passion."
Van's "There you are" (IX, 313) underlines her remark, which
sums up the weakness of the circle. Here, then, is form without
content, gesture without motion—the mark of a hollow, decadent
society.

Within this circle James creates characters alike in their modernity and their reliance on the head rather than the heart, but different in the ways in which they show their degeneration. Mrs.
Brook, the major figure, although her immorality is partly redeemed by her energy, her wit, her superiority, and her skill, is
nevertheless damned by her perversion of values—her sacrifice
of Nanda to her self-interest. Her intellectual supremacy disguises the grossness of her misdeeds, for even her scandalous
humiliation of Nanda at Tishy Grendon's, which is a brutal act
of personal violation, comes as the result of a carefully planned
and well executed intrigue.

One is tempted to admire if not condone Mrs. Brook because of
her intellectual as well as moral superiority to her foil, the
Duchess. Mrs. Brook and the Duchess play the same game, but
they use different rules. Mrs. Brook plots to marry Nanda to
Mitchy, and the Duchess tries to snare him for her niece, Little
Aggie. But the Duchess is deceptive and hypocritical, whereas
Mrs. Brook, for all her scheming, is above the vulgarity of the
Duchess's methods. The Duchess educates Aggie in the con-
tinental system; that is, she totally shelters her from her elders.
The Duchess feigns a complete devotion to Aggie, while Mrs.
Brook frankly admits that she has no interest in self-sacrifice. The
Duchess has an affair with Petherton; Mrs. Brook, though in love
with Vanderbank, does not have an affair with him.[37] The Duch-
ess's hypocrisy emerges in other ways also, for she schemes to
have Mitchy marry Aggie in order to acquire his fortune, though

she says that Mitchy, the son of a shoemaker, is beneath her social
level. She is hypocritical because she wishes to make Mrs. Brook
—who wants Mitchy for Nanda—feel unopposed. The Duchess's
methods are vulgarly blunt. Mrs. Brook tries to win Mitchy only
by suggesting tactfully to Nanda that she consider him, but the
Duchess, who never bothers to consider Aggie's desires—if she
has any—suggests that Mr. Longdon make it worth Van's while
to marry Nanda, virtually forces Mitchy to meet and talk with
Aggie, and compels her lover, Petherton, to praise Aggie's merits
("he must like *her*. Make him feel that he does" [IX, 115]).
Though the Duchess tells Mr. Longdon, "I can only work Mitchy
through Petherton, but Mrs. Brook can work him straight" (p.
254), she overestimates her adversary's vulgarity. Mrs. Brook
can work Mitchy straight, but she refuses to do so. Because of her
devotion to subtlety and wit, Mrs. Brook abhors bluntness, which
she associates with tastelessness; her method of keeping Van for
herself is indirect and relatively delicate, and her attempt to gain
Mitchy for Nanda recognizes limits of propriety. Even when she
is blunt—as when she makes herself hideous before Mr. Longdon
—her obvious behavior conceals a subtle method, since her intention is to appear so odious that Mr. Longdon will take Nanda.
Even Mrs. Brook's exposure of Nanda is less culpable than the
Duchess's cloistering of Aggie, because it is not only straightforward but also more beneficial to Nanda, who is allowed to know
in order to choose. The Duchess treats Aggie as a puppet, while
Mrs. Brook respects Nanda's mind and judgment.

Mrs. Brook also gains through contrast with Vanderbank, who
is a trimmer, capable of moral discrimination (Mitchy says,
"He's very much the best of us" [IX, 125]), but incapable of
converting his principles into action, and finally unable completely to break with Mrs. Brook's circle or completely to join it.
Vanderbank's personal drama is one of indecision. After months
of inconclusive consideration of Mr. Longdon's offer to marry
Nanda, Van finally withdraws, not because of his own decision but
because of Mrs. Brook's interference. Like the Duchess, Vanderbank represents a pseudo-traditionalism. For, as the Duchess pretends to follow an older code, Van is ultimately too old-fashioned
to condone Nanda's behavior. Mr. Longdon gives the lie to both

because, in his genuine traditionalism, he knows the difference
between the literal and the real, the overt and the actual. Thus
Van rejects Nanda because he suspects that she has been too exposed, though Mr. Longdon recognizes that Nanda's corruption
is superficial. He accepts Nanda as she is because he has the understanding to see through the appearances that prove a barrier
to Van. But Van's primary shortcoming is his pride—Mrs. Brook
terms him "awfully conceited and awfully patronising" (IX, 248)
—which Mrs. Brook exploits in order to stop him from marrying
her daughter. She tells Mitchy in Van's presence that Van "won't
want to have the pecuniary question mixed up with the matter:
to look in short as if he had had to be paid. He's like you, you
know—he's proud . . ." (IX, 300). Mrs. Brook thwarts Van; she
cleverly raises an issue that had heretofore been of secondary importance to him. Now he feels that to marry Nanda will damage
his reputation. Van's foil, Mitchy, has no such self-damaging
pride: out of devotion to Nanda he willingly makes himself appear a fool by marrying Aggie. Vanderbank is related to John
Marcher of "The Beast in the Jungle" in that he is incapable of
selfless love. Though Van is attracted to Nanda, he too readily
admits impediments, so that his own selfishness, masked as high
propriety, is the factor without which Mrs. Brook's interference
with Nanda would have been unsuccessful.

Mrs. Brook acquires stature when contrasted with the Duchess
and Van, but her basic immorality is most apparent when she is
contrasted with Nanda. Nanda resembles the other innocents of
James's London fiction. She is sealed up in a restricting environment; she is victimized by her parents; she has certain unattractive traits; and her positive action for good (her persuasion of
Mitchy to marry Aggie) creates evil. James belittles Nanda in the
beginning by showing that she suffers by contrast with both her
mother and her grandmother. She is not so worldly-wise as her
mother; she is not so good as her grandmother. Furthermore, she
is grim: "She's as bleak as a chimney-top when the fire's out" (IX,
452); she is also solemn: the jovial Mitchy never knows quite
what to make of her.

She is strangely old—older than her mother, even older than
Mr. Longdon—in her tragic awareness of things. She differs most

from her fellow heroines in that there is nothing romantic about
her; she is no victim of enchantment and has no illusions about
her world and her life. "What I am I must remain," she tells
Vanderbank; "I haven't what's called a principle of growth . . . .
I'm about as good as I can be—and about as bad. If Mr. Longdon
can't make me different nobody can" (IX, 214). She has inherited
her mother's uncanny perception, so that she knows from the beginning that she is fated to unhappiness: ". . . I shall be one of
the people who don't. I shall be at the end . . . one of those who
haven't" (IX, 232).

Like Maisie, Nanda has the talent for understanding what goes
on about her. Yet, unlike Maisie, she is prim and quaint rather
than pliable and fresh. She knows only disaster. She can reconcile neither joy nor good humor with her insight. However, her
perception shelters her from the intense personal grief that Isabel
Archer must live with and from the sudden shock of evil that
destroys Morgan Moreen. Nanda, after her mistreatment by her
mother and Van, is peculiarly calm; she even steals the scene as
she directs Van and Mitchy to comfort her mother. She is composed because she is inured to suffering and through experience
can bear the shock of reality which destroys her mother.

In spite of her acquaintance with her mother's group and Tishy
Grendon, Nanda is essentially innocent. Mr. Longdon realizes
that Nanda's differences from her grandmother are superficial and
environmental. Nanda tells him, "If [Lady Julia and I are] both
partly the result of other people, *her* other people were so different. . . . Granny wasn't the kind of girl she *could*n't be—and
so neither am I" (IX, 230–231). Forced against her will into her
mother's universe, thrown into association with Tishy Grendon so
that her mother might be free to live her own life (like the innocents of "The Turn of the Screw," Nanda is "blameless and foredoomed"), Nanda has in her awkward period developed a consciousness of reality that enables her to distinguish good and evil.
An irony of the novel is that although Van rejects Nanda for
knowing too much, it is only because of her knowledge that she
is able to achieve genuine, tested goodness. Her counterpart, Little Aggie, has the appearance of innocence; Nanda has the ap-

pearance of worldliness. Until her marriage, Aggie is an unknown quality:

> Decidedly [Aggie] was . . . an angel, and there was a wonder in her possession on this footing of one of the most expressive little faces that even her expressive race had ever shown. . . . Formed to express everything, it scarce expressed as yet even a consciousness. All the elements of play were in it, but they had nothing to play with (IX, 240).

Nanda's surface immorality corresponds to that of Maisie, whose initial approval of her elders shocks Mrs. Wix but disguises an innocence. Though Nanda may appear both grim and corrupted,[38] her very awareness and involvement support the moral sense, while Aggie, inexperienced, is immediately corrupted upon her introduction to the adult world. Thus Nanda's withdrawal contrasts with Aggie's entrance. It is a withdrawal prompted not only by devotion to Mr. Longdon and her mother—she feels obliged to do her part so that her mother may receive money from Mr. Longdon—but by her insistence on remaining free (Cashmore is ready to step in now that Van is out of the picture). Nanda's retreat is no renunciation, for she has nothing to renounce; yet in her final scenes with Van, Mitchy, and Mr. Longdon, she dramatizes the Jamesian doctrine that the self matures through knowledge of good and evil. Since she can have no personal happiness, she now devotes herself to patching the lives of others. When Nanda achieves full understanding of her situation, she loses self-consciousness. She has inherited the goodness of her grandmother; here she shows that she can put to proper use what she has learned from her mother. But when Nanda "squares" Van, Mitchy, Mr. Longdon, and even Mrs. Brook, her queenly control of others has a purity that comes from its total divorce from self-concern. Nanda's serenity, however, does not disguise the malignity of the world which she abandons. Her selflessness is an ironic contrast to the destructive egotism of her mother.

CHAPTER FOUR

Evil and the Major Phase

WHEN, in the first years of the twentieth century, James again took up the international theme, he used the same broad situation that had served him in the eighteen-seventies and eighties—the conflict of America and Europe against a European background. However, he so radically altered his treatment that his late international fiction must be considered not so much an extension of the earlier work as a distinct category. After the tightly restricted settings and unheroic protagonists of James's London novels, the international settings and international heroes of *The Ambassadors*, *The Wings of the Dove*, and *The Golden Bowl* significantly extend the scope of James's fiction. In the London fiction James was limited by subject matter and theme. The cramped Londoners with minor ambitions and, by comparison, petty problems, stand for man at his least heroic. The international theme offered James the setting for large-scale conflicts and characters of heroic dimensions.

Yet the novels of James's major phase are not so pointedly international as those of his earlier period. Not only do they contain little satire of American Puritanism and Philistinism, but also they stress moral rather than cultural differences.[1] It is significant, for example, that James planned *The Wings of the Dove* as a purely English novel.[2] Yet to provide his heroine with a moral strength that he found lacking in the English woman, he made Milly Theale an American. While Fleda Vetch and Nanda Brookenham are like the American heroines in their innocence and moral sense, they differ strikingly in being weak and unattractive. James looked to America to supply his heroines of stature, to complement morality with strength of character.

The American replaces the Londoner as hero because, at least potentially, he has the wisdom and the strength to survive in Europe. What is required for success is a maturing of the moral sense, an added perception, and a new power. It seems that James's own moral attitudes have changed with those of his heroes and heroines. The distance between Euphemia Cleve of the early "Madame de Mauves" and Maggie Verver of *The Golden Bowl* is as extreme as that between the Puritanical conception of morality which informs the first and the pragmatic conception which informs the second. Euphemia Cleve is virtue shocked and indignant at her husband's infidelity; she is adamant and unforgiving. Isabel Archer is disillusioned and hurt by Osmond, and like Euphemia she finds no alternative to sealing herself off from the world. Fleda Vetch marks a major deviation from this pattern: she cannot run away when she learns the truth about Mrs. Gereth, and tries to restore good. Maggie, like Euphemia and Isabel, finds herself betrayed and victimized. Unlike them, however, she does not withdraw. Like Fleda she combats the evil; but, unlike Fleda, she achieves high success.

For the American to counteract evil—and by doing so to retain a relationship with his immediate society—he must rise above the legalism of Puritanism and the squeamishness of innocence. The matured moral sense aligns itself with aspects of American life that James had either ignored or found wanting in America of the mid-nineteenth century. The new American is pliable. Isabel Archer lacks the rigidity of Euphemia Cleve and Gertrude Wentworth, but only to a point. She easily accepts cultural differences and welcomes new experience, to which she readily responds. But to the evil of Osmond and Mme. Merle Isabel reacts by rejecting the freedom which has brought her suffering. To the early James such renunciation represents high morality; to the late James it signifies a moral deficiency.

The later protagonists either possess or acquire an imagination which can penetrate surface facts and which can gain a transcendent understanding of things. Such an imagination rises above personal indignation and insistence on justice. James makes far greater demands upon native American idealism than he made in *The American* and *The Portrait of a Lady*. Positive virtue, such as that demonstrated by Maggie Verver, requires selflessness, a capacity for suffering, and a sense of social duty. The early heroines find their principal duty to be to themselves—to adhere unswervingly to their own ethical standards. The later heroines find their principal duty to be to others—to sacrifice themselves to the well-being of society.

The first requirement for the maintenance of a stable social relationship is the recognition of evil as an ineluctable condition of life. Furthermore, intelligence must be supported by resoluteness and resourcefulness. Up to *The Golden Bowl*, James's Americans are critically handicapped by their ignorance of the conditions of life. Even in *The Golden Bowl*, the innocent, Maggie Verver, is unaware of evil at the beginning of her European adventure, but once she gains her vision of evil, she uses her new insight to restore good, or at least to keep her marriage from collapsing. To lesser degrees and with less success, Lambert Strether and Milly Theale also acquire more than knowledge from their encounters with evil. Their knowledge enables, rather compels, them to *act*, and with considerable effectiveness. This is a new role for the Jamesian protagonist, whose characteristic tragic position has in the past been passivity.

Milly Theale uses the transcendent imagination to subdue evil. Though she dies a victim of treachery, her spiritual love for those who destroy her has the practical effect of converting an agent of evil to good. Maggie uses the transcendent imagination and the empirical intelligence to achieve both an ideal and a real triumph over those who have wronged her. James tends to associate both spiritual and intellectual power with wealth. (His inept Londoners are poor.) His Americans now have behind them not only the Puritan and Transcendental traditions, but also late nineteenth-century American financial strength. James vaguely identifies the American commercial empire with a native power that can produce not only the fortunes of the Newsomes, the Theales, and the Ververs, but also the deeds of spiritual and intellectual strength that enable Milly Theale and Maggie Verver to impede the evil of Europe.

Although James alters his picture of the American to include a greater generosity and a greater power, he seems to realize, far more than before, the American capacity for evil. With *The Ambassadors* he especially reveals the ugliness of American intolerance as well as the guilt that must accompany American wealth. With *The Wings of the Dove* he is concerned with the flaws of Milly Theale's innocence: her pride, her excessive reliance on money, and her hesitance to face life in its fullness. With *The Golden Bowl* he explores fully the underside of both American wealth and American innocence; the novel shows the essential destructiveness of imperception and immaturity. What was before often comic or pathetic becomes serious and tragic. In addition, James's later Americans prove not only extremely limited in themselves, but also menaces to the values and achievements of Europe.

Most of the malefactors in James's earlier international novels are impelled toward evil because their ambitions are social rather than private. For the sake of upholding a tradition, of adhering to a convention, or of maintaining a social position, they injure others. The evildoers of the late international novels are self-reliant; and, unlike the earlier Mme. Merle and Mrs. Brookenham, they neither adopt impersonal goals nor strive to satisfy external codes. James's late Europeans embody both national and personal qualities; they do not thoughtlessly conform to European mores. Maud Lowder of *The Wings of the Dove* belongs to the world of *The Awkward Age;* she is the British middle-class woman aspiring towards gentility. She stands alone in James's final international trilogy[3] as a European whose concern is primarily social. Mme. de Vionnet, Kate Croy, and Prince Amerigo surpass her in stature and dignity because they go beyond the demands of the world to seek a fulfillment that is personal.

Just as James's heroes and heroines become less legalistic and doctrinaire in their reactions to the evil of Europe, James himself shows hesitance to define and judge that evil. Evil in the novels of James's major phase is far more mysterious and ubiquitous than in his earlier works. The major reason is that it is less specifically linked to the sins of particular persons. Human differences, human weaknesses, and the complexity of life cause suffering and calamity, but the origin and the location of the evil are unspecified. In *The Golden Bowl,* in which each of the major figures contributes to the creation of the evil situation, the apparent source—the combined offenses of four people—seems disproportionate to the effects. Only in *The Wings of the Dove* is the crime terrible in itself. In *The Ambassadors* and *The Golden Bowl* there is neither an obvious crime nor an obvious villain, but the results of seemingly minor transgressions indicate that an extreme evil has been admitted to the scene. There is no superficial manifestation of villainy in the later novels. Furthermore, the offenders are as much as possible forgiven. Mme. de Vionnet, Kate Croy, and Charlotte Stant are placed in extremely difficult and compromising situations. To avoid the sins that they eventually commit would require a supreme virtue and a saintlike abnegation of happiness. Through his emphasis on the details of Kate Croy's background, James makes the reader sympathize with her, even though her plot against Milly Theale is inhumanly cruel. Likewise, since the American heroes do not apply their own moral codes dogmatically to the behavior of the Europeans, the effect is that James does not so much judge or condemn as simply reveal. Evil does not develop because of the sins of the malignant, but because of those of the weak. Yet the force of evil is not diminished; rather it is strengthened; for it is universal.

The agents of evil in the late novels remain aesthetically and intellectually fine specimens. The early villains have only a superficial and acquired attractiveness, which vanishes once they are found out. Yet Mme. de Vionnet actually gains charm and beauty when her sins are discovered; Kate Croy has a physical beauty and an intellectual strength which are not diminished by her monstrous crime; and Prince Amerigo epitomizes the grace of his ancestry. These characters have merits neither because of nor in spite of what they do. Unlike Sarah Pocock, Maud Lowder, and Fanny Assingham, the major evildoers are ladies and gentlemen whose dignity, charm, and good will are neither accidental nor superficial, but inherent in their natures. They are neither gross nor base; their being is separable from their behavior. James not only treats human character as far more complex than in his earlier works, but he also sees evil as far less explicable and identifiable. It is not removed or removable from human beings or human relationships, but no comfortable conclusions can be drawn about the evildoer. He is an agent of evil, but he is also much else.

In James's aesthetic sense of morality, all undesirable behavior is ugly, but with the later novels it is possible for one to be highly civilized and at the same time commit a great crime. In such case the sin is ugly, but the sinner remains beautiful. Mme. de Vionnet is genuinely beautiful—in an aesthetic and even a moral way—though she is the agent of an extreme evil. In respects other than her deception of Strether and intimacy with Chad, she has a high sense of responsibility and honor in human dealings. She is, as Strether recognizes, well worth saving.

Though it is not the only or even the main source of evil in James's late novels, deception is the most obvious cause of suffering. But this suffering does not consist simply of disillusion and resultant despair. The consciousness of the heroes and heroines is overwhelmed by mystery and confusion. The deceit of others combines with the mystery latent in Europe to create a severe anguish. With final knowledge there is disillusion and a more intense pain, but the dark journeys of James's protagonists do not end at this point, as do those of their predecessors. For Strether, Milly, and Maggie must continue to make their ways without retreat or the comfort of complete despair. Much of the obscurity in James's later works derives from the difficulty the characters have in going through the ordinary motions of life. One has the sense in reading *The Ambassadors, The Wings of the Dove,* and *The Golden Bowl*—especially the latter—that for a character to refer explicitly to the pressing situation that everyone is aware of but no one dares mention would be to shatter the lives of all. For the involved individuals to continue to live as social creatures, the evil that surrounds them must be kept from engulfing them. The indirection, nuances, and illusory surface calm of the later novels reflect the life of the novels. It is the struggle to preserve appearances that makes living a trial.

Behind James's emphasis on the importance of keeping up appearances—even though they directly contradict the reality of a situation—lies his recognition of the necessity of form—of manners. Though in the ideal society appearance and reality should correspond, one should preserve the appearance of the good and the beautiful even though it is an illusion. In 1908 James advised Edith Wharton to

> *go through the movements of life.* That keeps up our connection with life—I mean of the immediate and apparent life; behind which, all the while, the deeper and darker and unapparent, in which things *really* happen to us, learns, under that hygiene, to stay in its place. Let it get out of its place and it swamps the scene; besides which its place, God knows, is enough for it![4]

Latent and suppressed evil is more terrible than overt evil. But, paradoxically, evil must be concealed if there is to be any basis for living.

The appearance of life is not the full or even the adequate life; it makes deception, hypocrisy, insincerity, and artificiality inevitable. In his grasping for a workable relationship between individual and society, James rejects the simple solution of renunciation—the abandonment of social relationships out of ethical scruple—and shows the necessity of a stoic endurance of things as they are. Also, appearances have a reality of their own. For James, style and manners, as well as surface humanity and recognition of basic amenities, are prerequisites for civilization. They are not enough to relieve isolation, but they provide grounds for social intercourse.

The late novels are really about the disintegration of western civilization. They reflect what James's letters and notebooks frequently state—his vision of "this overwhelming, self-defeating chaos or cataclysm toward which the whole thing is drifting."[5] One way of defining James's ideal of civilization is to say that not only should society offer the individual a contact with the aesthetic and social values of history—art and manners—but also that these values must be consistent with actual human behavior. In the late novels Americans and Europeans alike undermine and at the same time struggle to maintain the values of the past. Forms, surfaces, and manners have become all but incompatible with the human standards they should ideally reflect.

In *The Ambassadors, The Wings of the Dove,* and *The*

Golden Bowl, James varies slightly his dominant theme of appearance and reality to dramatize his vision of the American-European world straining to preserve itself from internal destruction. Appearance, the historical heritage of art and manners, is no longer reality: at best it is a thin disguise lending meretricious splendor to a behavior alien to it; at worst it is a thing to be kept in museums, a refuge from reality. The reality of greed, with its mechanics of intrigue and duplicity, seeks the appearance of art and manners. There is a consistent dichotomy between the form and the content of civilization, between past and present, between society and individual. When the form collapses, society becomes anarchy and merely the sum-total of individual grasping egos. The value of the form is ambiguous, for it adds the horror of deceit to the evil of economic and human plunder; but also it is a restraint: it provides a uniformity of standards and a social cohesiveness without which there would be no community at all. Society and civilization collapse together when Strether sees the duplicity of Mme. de Vionnet and Chad, and when Lord Mark reveals Densher's plot to Milly. In *The Golden Bowl* Maggie Verver has her vision of reality, but instead of withering she struggles successfully to maintain appearances. But in *The Ambassadors* and *The Wings of the Dove*, the perceptions of Strether and Milly of the hollowness of form bring about the death of civilization.

Such are the Jamesian moments of exclusion, in which the individual finds himself isolated, unsupported by values outside of himself, unable to define himself through his social and historical position. The nature of the relationship between the innocent seeker and the cultured world of experience has significantly changed since a novel like *The Portrait of a Lady*. Isabel Archer's problem is to reconcile the values of a traditional society with her personal ideals. At opposite poles are Henrietta Stackpole, whose limitations are measured by her absolute hostility to Europe, and Mme. Merle, who is morally deficient because she lives "exclusively for the world" (IV, 144). Mme. Merle tells Isabel, "There's no such thing as an isolated man or woman; we're each of us made up of some cluster of appurtenances" (III, 287). The novel reveals the need for synthesis between the personal and the social code.

The norm is clearly Ralph Touchett, who appreciates the need for "appurtenances" to the self—that is why he persuades his father to make Isabel rich—and yet is ultimately self-reliant in his moral judgments. In the world of a novel like *The Wings of the Dove*, however, no such compromise is possible. Thus the moral person is forced back on himself, denied any kind of meaningful social relationship. James's last novels treat the dual movements of society's dissolution and the individual's recognition of his essential isolation. They dramatize the reality of evil overcoming the appearance of beauty.

THE AMBASSADORS

In *The Ambassadors* James fully achieves what he had approached in many of his earlier works: the identification of action with vision. Although the protagonist, Lambert Strether, is one of James's spectator heroes, he is not held back from life by the debility of a Ralph Touchett or the intellectual pride of a Vanderbank. In the person of Strether vision is action; it represents a full participation in experience. It is dynamic, dramatic, and personal.

Strether's relation with Europe is dynamic and dramatic because it is personal. Strether is in Europe as the emissary of Mrs. Newsome, who has sent him from Woollett, Massachusetts, in order to retrieve her son, Chad, whom she and the rest of Woollett suspect to have become involved with a disreputable French woman. When he arrives in Europe, Strether carries with him a strong sense of obligation to fulfill his mission; and he also holds the Woollett attitude toward Paris. He believes it to be a modern Babylon, in which Chad has been seduced into the conventional and vulgar vices. Moreover, Strether is motivated by more than a sense of duty. His future happiness depends upon his success in bringing Chad home. Strether, a widower in his mid-fifties, has obtained neither wealth nor success. He is a friend to the Newsome family and for years has edited the literary magazine which the wealthy and influential Mrs. Newsome has subsidized. Strether has reason to believe that Mrs. Newsome will marry him if he is successful as her ambassador to Europe. Therefore, even though Strether is almost entirely a spectator, he is personally involved in the situation he observes.

James traces the development of Strether's understanding of a particular Parisian social group. Before Strether sees Chad, he discovers the beauty of Paris: its cultural, aesthetic, and architectural richness, which indicates a way of life more satisfying than that of Woollett. Even before he meets Chad, his prejudices begin to be modified, and after he meets Chad they all but vanish. James dramatizes Strether's awakening in visual terms. Strether "sees" truth: in the architecture of Chad's home and in Chad's appearance in a theater box. Each successive impression forces Strether to shift his moral position, to consider the relation of the new impression to his duty to Mrs. Newsome; by seeing one thing differently he is made to see other things differently.

Midway in the novel Strether, in the process of comparing the life of his new Parisian friends to his own starved past and equally bleak future, reveals to Little Bilham, Chad's companion, the startling influence of Paris on him. In his advice to Bilham to "live," Strether shows his realization of his own situation ("It's too late" [XXI, 217]). Now unable to live actively and immediately, he can live passively and remotely. He is not, however, experiencing life merely vicariously. Through seeing and through understanding, he does "have his life." In Strether's mind, scenes create impressions and impressions give rise to insights.

Strether must deal with two kinds of evil: the evil of Europe and the evil of America. His growth involves a rejection of the evils of America which he has brought with him to Europe and an acceptance of the evils of Europe which he gradually discovers. To achieve self-fulfillment, he must cast off the American evils of prejudice, intolerance, narrowness, and smugness. James exposes Puritanism in *The Ambassadors* not only through Jim and Sarah Pocock and the felt presence of Mrs. Newsome, but also through Strether himself, who gradually abandons the worst aspects of his Puritan heritage. In the beginning his fault is simply his ignorance and his prejudices; he accepts without serious consideration the Woollett view of Paris and of Chad. Even when he realizes the fallacy of such notions, he still retains subtler but equally dangerous traits of New England Puritanism.

In *The Ambassadors* James equates the New England fear of experience with evil. He delves into the psychological basis of the

New England conscience and its related evils by showing them
to be manifestations of a fear of the unknown. For such a New
Englander as Waymarsh the foreign is to be feared and hated because it is unknown. Thus, comically but significantly, Waymarsh
becomes shocked and fearful when, early in the novel, Strether
begins to make casual advances into European life. The purchase
of a pair of gloves in a British shop portends horrors to Waymarsh:

> Mere discriminations about a pair of gloves could . . . rep-
> resent . . . possibilities of something that Strether could
> make a mark against only as the peril of apparent wantonness.
> He had quite the consciousness of his new friend [Maria
> Gostrey], for their companion, that he might have had of
> a Jesuit in petticoats, a representative of the recruiting inter-
> ests of the Catholic Church. The Catholic Church, for Way-
> marsh—that was to say the enemy, the monster of bulging
> eyes and far-reaching quivering groping tentacles—was
> exactly society, exactly the discrimination of types and tones,
> exactly the wicked old Rows of Chester, rank with feuda-
> lism; exactly in short Europe (XXI, 41).

Strether is the only New Englander who can accept his fear of
the unknown as a fear, instead of converting it into a rigid antagonism, justified on flimsy moral grounds. In the beginning he can
admit to Maria Gostrey his dread of his forthcoming adventure:
"I'm always considering something else; something else, I mean,
than the thing of the moment. The obsession of the other thing is
the terror" (XXI, 19). Strether's honest attempt to discover truth
without a priori judgments involves a painful conquest of his fear
of life. With the other ambassadors, there is no such honesty.

What appears quaintly provincial in *The Europeans* becomes
aggressive and dangerous in *The Ambassadors*. The Wentworth
family is rendered by its Calvinistic heritage incapable of moral
maturity because it is unable to absorb new experience. In *The
Ambassadors* James views New England Puritanism, coupled
with the force of New England industrial power, as capable of a
greater evil. What is ignorance in the Wentworths becomes intolerance in the Pococks. New England loses the dignity of its mid-

nineteenth-century patriarchal society and replaces it by the in-
humanity of its late-century commercialism.

Strether is saved from being a complete New Englander by his
imagination and by his lack of economic and social success. Unable to participate fully in New England wealth and culture,
Strether partly escapes its deadening effects, so that his wisdom
is allowed, if not to grow, to remain latent until Europe can nur-
ture it. Mrs. Newsome, the Pococks, and Waymarsh, however,
like many of James's morally deficient Americans and Europeans, allow their personal attitudes to be replaced by pervasive
regional or cultural attitudes. Accordingly, Mrs. Newsome's
dominant trait is her inflexibility.

James's exposure of Puritanism as a malignant force is equivalent to linking ignorance with sin. Maria Gostrey tells Strether
that Sarah Pocock's vilification ("Do you consider her even an
apology for a decent woman?" [XXII, 202]) of Mme. de Vionnet
cannot be justified by ignorance. "She imagined meanly," she tells
Strether. "He had it, however, better. 'It couldn't but be ignorantly.' 'Well, intensity with ignorance—what do you want
worse?' " (XXII, 225). In themselves ignorance and fear are
merely negative deficiencies, but in practice they lead directly to
the kind of dynamic intolerance which the later James sees as the
source of a far greater evil than Europe.

In the early chapters of *The Ambassadors*, James stresses the
baseness of American capitalism. The Newsome fortune far ex-
ceeds that of the earlier Christopher Newman, whose methods of
acquisition, while perhaps undignified, were never unethical. In
speaking with Maria Gostrey about the Newsome fortune,
Strether says, "The source of [Chad's] grandfather's wealth—and
thereby of his own share in it—was not particularly noble" (XXI,
62). A bit later, Strether refers to the manner in which Mrs. Newsome uses her wealth: ". . . her money is spent, her life conceived and carried on with a large beneficence." Maria's reply is
immediate and devastating (she dares constantly to mention
realities which Strether shies from considering): "That's a kind
of expiation of wrongs" (XXI, 63).

Just as Mrs. Newsome and Sarah Pocock embody the brute
strength of American wealth, so Jim Pocock and Waymarsh

manifest its crippling effect. Waymarsh and Jim Pocock, unlike
the earlier Mr. Ruck, the business man in "The Pension Beaurepas," are not simply pathetic. Though they are comic in their
vulgarity and their inability to enjoy Europe, they are not simply
victims of a fierce economic system, but are so emotionally and
morally deranged by their backgrounds that they have become
agents of evil. Waymarsh, whose provincialism is at first comic,
emerges in the course of the novel as sinister. His distorted sense
of values and perverted notion of duty cause him to betray his
friendship to Strether by surreptitiously reporting his activities
to Mrs. Newsome and by callously siding with the Pococks. Jim
Pocock, whose lack of dignity and moral stature is partly a result
of his own business activities and partly of his domination by the
women of the Newsome household, lacks the ethical rigidity of
his wife and mother-in-law, but he is equally repulsive because
of his coarseness. Jim Pocock is the American business man
blighted and dehumanized, made bestial through his activity in
industry. He is an enemy of the fine and the noble. His raucous
delight in a Paris which he imagines a center of licentiousness and
debauchery is but the counterpart of his wife's prejudiced denun-
ciation of Paris. As Van Wyck Brooks notes, "Jim Pocock's face
is the same face of horror that Spencer Brydon ["The Jolly
Corner"] encountered when the ghost of his American self
dropped its hands." [6] Brydon, like Abel Gaw of *The Ivory Tower*,
has been turned into a monster by his life of commerce.[7]

Enabled to profit from a new experience because of his incomplete connection with Woollett, Strether gradually acquires a new
set of values. Initially Strether learns of the positive values of Europe and of the evils of Woollett; later he learns of the evils of
Europe. His first major step is his liberation from the narrow-
mindedness of New England: an evil and dangerous tendency to
condemn the foreign. Strether gradually replaces condemnation
by suspicion, and finally judgment by sympathy. Before he even
meets Chad, he has learned through acquaintance with his friends
and his surroundings that his preconceived notions were false and
oversimplified. He can honestly reconsider his position: "He must
approach Chad, must wait for him, deal with him, master him,

but he mustn't dispossess himself of the faculty of seeing things as they were" (XXI, 118). Strether proceeds cautiously, and he begins to realize the necessity for making distinctions undreamed of in Woollett. By observing the remarkable and beneficial alteration in Chad, who has gained a culture and a refinement far superior to that of the New Englander, Strether recognizes that he is dealing not with the broad caricature of Paris and of "life" that Woollett accepts as fact, but with a complex, subtle phenomenon that has much of value and nothing of vulgarity. Strether realizes that "to live" is certainly not to be evil in the Woollett sense of the word: "experience was what Chad did play on him, if he didn't play any grossness of defiance. Of course experience was in a manner defiance; but it wasn't, at any rate—rather indeed quite the contrary!—grossness; which was so much gained" (XXI, 155).

Strether's readjustment represents a rejection of personal pride —a pride that justifies fear and ignorance. His moral aid to Chad and Mme. de Vionnet requires self-surrender. When he decides to renounce the happiness and security promised by Mrs. Newsome to "save" Chad and Mme. de Vionnet, he tells Maria Gostrey, "I seem to have a life only for other people" (XXI, 269). In spite of his personal renunciation, however, Strether retains up to the very end of his experience some dangerous New England traits. Like the governess of "The Turn of the Screw," he is capable of asking unpleasant and compromising questions in order to justify his own behavior. He questions Bilham as to the precise nature of the relation between Chad and Mme. de Vionnet, demanding to know whether it is a "virtuous attachment" (XXI, 181). Later he questions Miss Barrace about Mme. de Vionnet: "Will you answer me a plain question? Will she ever divorce?" (XXI, 265). It becomes clear from Strether's more mature behavior at the conclusion of his experience, when he acquires the taste to respect the dignity of others and the imagination to perceive the fallacy of judging from the obvious, that such legalistic probings are tainted with pride.

Strether becomes attracted to Europe for aesthetic reasons. He rejects his New England morality not because he encounters a

superior morality in Europe, but because he recognizes the shortsightedness of the conventional Woollett evaluation of Europe.
He sides with Europe rather than with America because he is
greatly impressed by European beauty. Strether errs in making
an unconscious equation between art and morality: first, he applies New England principles to European life, and later, after he
has repudiated Mrs. Newsome, he tends to see aesthetic grace as a
kind of morality in itself. Not till the end of his adventure does
Strether realize the proper relationship between art and morality,
when he finds that evil is an attribute of beauty.

Because Strether is a spectator rather than a participant and because his vision is his major faculty, his viewpoint is mainly aesthetic. As his perception increases and more things come into its
ken, he discovers the true content of beauty. Strether first "sees"
Chad, in terms of art, as an "irreducible young pagan" (XXI,
156–157). But Strether is betrayed by his vision, for while he is
vastly pleased by the bearing of Chad, he is blinded by the surface to the moral essence of Chad. Strether realizes much later
that Chad is a pagan—i. e., faithless, capricious, materialistic—
in reality as well as in appearance. Thus Strether too casually dismisses his original fears about Chad. Although Strether thinks of
Chad's new manner as smooth, he overlooks the implications of
superficiality in the term.

Strether's renunciation of Woollett occurs at the crucial scene
in Gloriani's garden, in which Strether is introduced to the splendor of Parisian culture and is so impressed that he urges Bilham to
experience life to its fullest. Here is life as art—in the scene itself,
in Gloriani, and especially in Mme. de Vionnet. At the beginning
of the party, Strether is painfully conscious of his "odious ascetic
suspicion of any form of beauty" (XXI, 193–194), but in the
course of the afternoon he all but completely dispels this Calvinistic hostility.

The scene in Gloriani's garden occurs in a carefully delineated
setting, which is filtered through Strether's consciousness in a
series of impressions which suggest that there is more to Parisian
culture than simply beauty. Thus, as Strether gains a panoramic
impression of the area about the garden, he thinks of it in religious terms:

> Strether had presently the sense of a great convent, a convent
> of missions, famous for he scarce knew what, a nursery of
> young priests, of scattered shade, of straight alleys and
> chapel-bells, that spread its mass in one quarter; he had the
> sense of names in the air, of ghosts at the windows, of signs
> and tokens, a whole range of expression, all about him, too
> thick for prompt discrimination (XXI, 196).

Strether has the sense of being initiated into the old and the
beautiful. But the curious image of "a nursery of young priests"[8]
suggests that Strether considers his approaching experience with
Europe as both a retreat from the mediocrity and anxiety of the
world and an introduction to an ideal condition of innocence. It
is a mark of Strether's inexperience that he believes the aesthetic
life to be a sanctuary from all forms of evil.

Immediately after this "assault of images" (XXI, 196), Strether
is introduced to Gloriani himself, the complete European aesthete,
and in the scene James continues to suggest the inseparability of
beauty from evil. After observing Gloriani, Strether realizes that
beneath the fine surface culture of the artist there is something of
the fierce and the terrible. When he sees Gloriani in conversation
with a duchess, he receives a distinct impression:

> Were they, this pair, of the "great world"?—and was he
> himself, for the moment and thus related to them by his ob-
> servation, *in* it? Then there was something in the great world
> covertly tigerish, which came to him across the lawn and in
> the charming air as a waft from the jungle. Yet it made him
> admire most of the two, made him envy, the glossy male
> tiger, magnificently marked (XXI, 219).

Strether associates the sensuousness of the artist with the sensuousness of the man. The image of the tiger stands for sexual passion.
Gloriani symbolizes the whole of European culture, and, as physical beauty is inseparable from sexual energy in him, the same is
true of Europe as a whole, and particularly of Mme. de Vionnet,
the embodiment of its beauty.

Strether's sudden and only half-conscious perception of Gloriani is but a short-lived awareness. He reverts to idealizing the aesthetic life of Europe without accepting its suggested components.

Such life, Strether eventually realizes, is associated not with a retreat from reality, but with elements of reality that he finds unpleasant. When Strether urges Bilham to "have your life," he is only partly aware of the implication of his statement.

Strether still harbors dim suspicions of Mme. de Vionnet's guilt and Chad's deception. He is not yet morally prepared for total knowledge. It is ironic that when Strether finally does accept unreservedly the cause of Chad and Mme. de Vionnet, he does so in true Woollett fashion: he believes he has evidence of their innocence. When he sees Mme. de Vionnet in Notre Dame Cathedral he naïvely reasons:

> [Mme. de Vionnet's] attitude fitted admirably into the stand
> he had privately taken about her connexion with Chad on the
> last occasion of his seeing them together. It helped him to
> stick fast at the point he had then reached; it was there he
> had resolved that he *would* stick, and at no moment since
> had it seemed as easy to do so. Unassailably innocent was a
> relation that could make one of the parties to it so carry her-
> self. If it wasn't innocent why did she haunt the churches?
> —into which, given the woman he could believe he made
> out, she would never have come to flaunt an insolence of
> guilt (XXII, 10).

Strether here projects New England attitudes toward religion and morality. Nevertheless his tacit pledge of loyalty is a sincere one, and it enables him to withstand the shocks that follow, when he discovers that the relationship between Chad and Mme. de Vionnet is sexual.

Preliminary to his discovery of the nature of the relationship, Strether learns from Mme. de Vionnet that she is planning a marriage for Jeanne, her daughter. Up to this point, Strether, convinced of Chad's innocence, has believed that Jeanne and Chad will eventually marry. The sudden knowledge shocks him. He feels the oppression of the "cold chambers of the past" (XXII, 127), of a way of life which allows the prearranged marriage and condones a union not entirely innocent between a married woman and a younger man. He has the sense of "being further and further 'in'" (XXII, 127–128), of being "concerned in something

deep and dim. He had allowed for depths, but these were greater
. . . . It was—through something ancient and cold in it—what
he would have called the real thing" (XXII, 129).

Most significant in Strether's development is that after receiv-
ing the information about Jeanne from Mme. de Vionnet, he replies, "How *much* I have to judge!" (XXII, 131). The comment
indicates that though Strether has gone far, he has still farther to
go. He must renounce judging entirely. Though it will entail
extreme suffering and involve painful self-effacement, he must
accept reality as it is, for he will soon be called upon to exercise
a sympathy and an understanding utterly incompatible with the
pride which allows one to judge his fellow man.

Strether's experience is one of developing awareness: of
beauty, of history, of culture. For his experience to be complete
his perception must be all-inclusive. Therefore he must come to a
knowledge of evil. Since all his knowledge has been acquired
through seeing, it is appropriate and significant that his perception
of evil be literally visual. Journeying through the countryside
near Paris, Strether stops at an inn, and, while sitting in the garden, he notices Chad and Mme. de Vionnet together in a boat.
When they come to shore and join Strether in dinner, it becomes
apparent that they have planned to spend the night in the inn. In
handling the scene in which Strether discovers the intimacy between Chad and Mme. de Vionnet, James reveals that the incident, along with its implications, points to the essential nature of
European culture. The incident is a part which stands for the
whole. As Strether begins his short journey, he is intent upon
discovering a pastoral scene "that would remind him of a certain
small Lambinet that had charmed him, long years before, at a
Boston dealer's and that he had quite absurdly never forgotten"
(XXII, 245). He happens upon a landscape that fills the require-
ments. Thus Strether, at the time of the excursion seeking art in
life, is most conscious of the aesthetic side of Europe. The limits
of his vision provide the framework of a painting. Viewing the
river, he finds a harmony usually found only in art. When his
revery is disturbed by the sight of the couple in the boat, his perception of Europe becomes complete. Beauty and truth become
one. Neither Strether nor the reader is allowed to dissociate the

ugly from the beautiful, for both are essential to Europe. The
harmony of Strether's projected canvas is not destroyed but completed and deepened.

Strether, Maria Gostrey tells us, possesses "treasures of imagination" (XXII, 225), a power of mind capable of transcending
prejudices and surfaces to a knowledge of reality. In the pastoral
scene he exercises the faculty which enables him to see that Europe is neither simply good nor simply evil, but something which
contains both, a luxuriant complexity in which life approaches
art but remains life. He reconciles what had been the conflicting
opposites of moral reality and aesthetic reality, and creates a unity
that transcends both.[9] Strether's adventure is virtually ended, for
it has been a drama of the expanding consciousness; and when it
encounters the ugly and the evil, it assimilates them with the
beautiful and the good. The result is not a less valuable awareness,
but a more valuable one, for it is complete.

The Ambassadors does not end when Strether discovers that
the relationship between Chad and Mme. de Vionnet is not "a
virtuous attachment." Strether has further dealings with the participants, and his final attitude toward Mme. de Vionnet especially suggests the redemptive effect of his full and complex
vision—of which evil is an essential component—upon his moral
character. Strether's involvement in the affairs of Chad and Mme.
de Vionnet has been personal, not only because he has sacrificed
the advantages of Woollett in order to defend Chad, but also because his sympathy and affection, especially for Mme. de Vionnet,
have acted as a bond, connecting his life with hers. In his effort to
"save" her, he has become attached in an essential way to the life
she represents. When he discovers her intimacy with Chad, he
does not sever himself from her, but accepts the evil of which she
is an agent as endemic to the world in which she lives. Initial
shock and disillusion are replaced by a kind of sober recognition
of universal human frailty. While walking the streets of Paris and
posting a letter, Strether thinks of his close identification with the
city and with what it now represents to him:

> After he had put in his paper he had ranged himself, he was
> really amused to think, on the side of the fierce, the sinister,

the acute. He was carrying on a correspondence, across the great city, quite in the key of the *Postes et Télégraphes* in general; and it was fairly as if the acceptance of that fact had come from something in his state that sorted with the occupation of his neighbors. He was mixed up with the typical tale of Paris, and so were they, poor things—how could they all together help being? They were no worse then he, in short, and he no worse then they—if, queerly enough, no better. . . .

. . . if he lived on thus with the sinister from hour to hour it proved an easier thing than one might have supposed in advance. He reverted in thought to his old tradition, the one he had been brought up on and which even so many years of life had but little worn away; the notion that the state of the wrongdoer, or at least this person's happiness, presented some special difficulty. What struck him now rather was the ease of it—for nothing in truth appeared easier (XXII, 271–272).

In his final scene with Mme. de Vionnet, Strether not only refuses to judge her, but also displays an overriding sympathy that amounts to a kind of love. While earlier he had helped Mme. de Vionnet in order to repay her for what she had done for Chad ("a criterion savoring of Woollett," as F. W. Dupee remarks),[10] now he helps her because she needs Chad. And Strether's desperate efforts to prevent Chad from deserting her attest his devotion to her.

The nature of the evil of Europe is less explicit in *The Ambassadors* than in any other James novel. Far clearer is the evil of Woollett. It is ironic that even though Mrs. Newsome and Sarah Pocock are right in believing their suspicions of adultery to be well founded, they are no less immoral for their condemnation of Strether and Mme. de Vionnet. They are wrong not only in their prejudices and in their blindness to beauty, but also in their unequivocal and easy identification of adultery with evil and in their condemnation of the adulterer. Before his initiation into Europe, Strether possesses the typical New England attitudes toward physical passion. In the process of his awakening—once he is convinced that Chad's affair is pure—he tends to ignore the existence of passion. But in the meantime he has become so impressed with the superior humanity of Mme. de Vionnet that even the shock which reveals her to be engaged in adultery cannot erase the previous image.

In effect James treats the adultery without ethical consideration, for he, like Strether, refuses to judge. He does, however, link the adultery with ugliness, but an ugliness that resides solely in the illicit passion and not in the participants. To both James and Strether, adultery is as coarse as it is to Woollett; yet the adulterers themselves are not coarse. Thus, what Strether had observed earlier in Gloriani—a combination of aesthetic beauty and sexual energy—he finds also in Mme. de Vionnet. Eventually Strether realizes the inseparability of the sensuous and the sensual in Paris.

Mme. de Vionnet is further exculpated because James treats her love for Chad as almost beyond her control, so that she is more a victim of sin than a sinner. In his final scene with her, Strether finds that she regrets and despises the weakness which causes her to love Chad:

> "What I hate is myself—when I think that one has to take so much, to be happy, out of the lives of others, and that one isn't happy even then. . . . The wretched self is always there, always making one somehow a fresh anxiety. What it comes to is that it's not, that it's never, a happiness, any happiness at all, to *take*" (XXII, 282–283).

Mme. de Vionnet is pathetic not only in her painful self-knowledge and unhappiness, but also in her dependence on Chad. The sympathy that James displays for her in her sorrow and abjection is a sympathy for man's weakness and human suffering. Maria Gostrey has the last word on the situation: "I'm sorry for us all" (XXII, 303).

Just as the evil and ugliness of adultery are transcended by the personal beauty of Mme. de Vionnet, in the same way her deception of Strether is transcended by the manner in which she deceives him. Strether understands that "their eminent 'lie,' Chad's and hers, was simply after all such an inevitable tribute to good taste as he couldn't have wished them not to render . . . . That

is he could trust her to make deception right. As she presented
things the ugliness—goodness knows why—went out of them
. . ." (XXII, 277). It is not simply that Mme. de Vionnet's grace
excuses her behavior or that she is led to deceive Strether because
of an uncontrollable passion, but that the deception itself, though
it amounts to a betrayal of Strether and causes him suffering, is an
inevitable effect of the original evil—the adultery. Certainly
Mme. de Vionnet and Chad gain Strether's favor under false pre-
tenses; yet Strether's original prejudice was at least equally
wrong. Maria Gostrey, in effect, deceives Strether by not telling
him the truth about Chad and Mme. de Vionnet, which she has
known from the beginning. But, as Strether ultimately realizes,
immediate knowledge of the literal facts would have meant to
him "a revulsion in favour of the principles of Woollett" (XXII,
296). Maria saves Strether from spiritual decay by deceiving him.
Bilham lies to him when Strether blatantly asks him whether
Chad's friendship is innocent. Strether justifies Bilham's deception
through appreciation of the superior morality of loyalty and
prudence ("Little Bilham had lied like [a gentleman]" [XXII,
299]). Strether defends the admitted evil of Mme. de Vionnet's
deception by seeing it as an act of "good taste." The forms of
civilization are worth preserving at all costs. Once a situation is
grounded in evil, other evils must follow. In *The Ambassadors*,
Strether himself, by abetting an adultery—at first ignorantly and
then knowingly—commits himself to making the best of a corrupt situation. Strether chooses the complexity of beauty and
ugliness in Europe for the sake of beauty. Therefore Mme. de
Vionnet's deception has the ultimate effect of saving, albeit temporarily, a valuable though imperfect mode of life and of allowing
Strether to have his life. Beyond this, James and his mature characters recognize the value of appearances and of keeping the evil
hidden beneath the surfaces. Strether's accidental discovery prevents a successful containment of evil, and after his discovery,
when the evil comes to the surface, a civilization dies. Shame,
sorrow, and revulsion do not replace but become fused with
grace and beauty.
  Strether's experience amounts to a discovery of the fullness of
life, for Europe itself, which embodies the deeds of man at his

finest and of man at his worst, provides not merely a special kind
of experience and an enriching one, but an experience without
which one is incomplete. James uses Mme. de Vionnet as a personal symbol of Europe—its past, its art, its complexity, its mystery, its evil. She is identified pictorially with Europe. When he
first visits Mme. de Vionnet, Strether finds

> himself making out, as a background of the occupant, some
> glory, some prosperity of the First Empire, some Napoleonic
> glamour, some dim lustre of the great legend; elements cling-
> ing still to all the consular chairs and mythological brasses
> and sphinxes' heads and faded surfaces of satin striped with
> alternate silk (XXI, 244).

As here she is associated with the First Empire, at other times
she is linked to the Renaissance, an association especially suggestive of the aesthetic wealth of the past: "Her head, extremely fair
and exquisitely festal, was like a happy fancy, a notion of the
antique, on an old precious medal, some silver coin of the Renaissance . . ." (XXI, 270). The allusion to the Renaissance leads directly to a more remote antiquity: "He could have compared her
to a goddess still partly engaged in a morning cloud, or to a sea-
nymph waist-high in the summer surge" (XXI, 270).

James associates the grace and beauty, along with the mystery,
of Mme. de Vionnet with the Renaissance and the tradition of
classical art. In both periods of history there are connotations of
sensuality which James subtly invokes in order to achieve an
additional connection between Mme. de Vionnet and her heritage.
But the evil that vaguely lurks about Mme. de Vionnet and her
situation is more often related, scenically and metaphorically, to
the period of the First French Empire, which suggests to James
violence and horror. On one occasion, when Strether takes his
leave from Mme. de Vionnet's rooms, he gains a startling impression: "He stopped, he looked back; the whole thing made a vista,
which he found high melancholy and sweet—full, once more, of
dim historic shades, of the faint far-away cannon-roar of the
great Empire" (XXII, 125). The sense of Paris, of the evil of its
past, permeates the novel, and toward the end of his experience
Strether is especially aware of the closeness of the evil of the past.

The streets and buildings of Paris remain beautiful and picturesque, but they suggest the darkness as well as the light of the
past, particularly of the period of the revolution:

> Strether had all along been subject to sudden gusts of fancy
> in connexion with such matters as these—odd starts of the
> historic sense, suppositions and divinations with no warrant
> but their intensity. Thus and so, on the eve of the great re-
> corded dates, the days and nights of revolution, the sounds
> had come in, the omens, the beginnings broken out. They
> were the smell of revolution, the smell of the public temper
> —or perhaps simply the smell of blood (XXII, 274).

In spite of his ultimate revelation, there is still much that remains mysterious to Strether. He has his facts and he has his impressions, but his logic and ethics are powerless to reconcile them
in any intelligible way. He can do nothing but accept his vision
as truth. Through his own experience he has met but not penetrated the mystery of the past, and he can feel but awe and contribute but sympathy. Soon after his arrival, while conversing
with some of Chad's friends, Strether feels that "Nothing . . .
could well less resemble a scene of violence than even the liveliest
of these occasions" (XXI, 173). He is yet to learn that the violence of the past still exerts an influence in the most superficially
innocuous and casual scenes and occasions. With his imaginative
ability to see beyond the literal, Strether can associate Mme. de
Vionnet and his entire experience not simply with the beauty of
the past, but also with its evil. In his last interview with Mme. de
Vionnet, Strether sees her

> dressed as for thunderous times, and it fell in with the kind
> of imagination we have just attributed to him that she should
> be in simplest coolest white, of a character so old-fashioned,
> if he were not mistaken, that Madame Roland must on the
> scaffold have worn something like it . . . . The associations
> of the place . . . were at first as delicate as if they had been
> ghostly . . . . He knew in advance he should look back on
> the perception actually sharpest with him as on the view of
> something old, old, old, the oldest thing he had ever per-
> sonally touched . . . (XXII, 275–276).

At the very end, Strether "felt what he had felt before with her, that there was always more behind what she showed, and more and more again behind that" (XXII, 283).

The evil of Europe then is ultimately indefinable, but its effects are concrete and definite, especially in the acute suffering of all the persons who are affected by it. The conclusion of the novel stresses suffering. Strether's final deed is an effort to prevent Chad from deserting Mme. de Vionnet. Chad, in spite of the surface culture which he has acquired through intimacy with Mme. de Vionnet, lacks the dignity and nobility of her character. He deserts her because she is old and exposed and because his own interests lie in the gross materialism of Woollett and in another woman. Mme. de Vionnet's tragedy is that she is too fine for Chad, who, unlike Strether, is incapable of appreciating her, and yet too dependent on him, for she cannot endure the loss of him. She is weak and mortal humanity, redeemed by beauty and grace.

THE WINGS OF THE DOVE

The Wings of the Dove (1902) [11] treats a later stage in the collapse of western civilization than *The Ambassadors*.[12] *The Ambassadors* deals with the last gasping breath of the old order; by the time of *The Wings* the old order is dead, visible only in its decay. Strether is the last Jamesian pilgrim to gain a relationship with what James has termed the "*visitable* past," [13] as Mme. de Vionnet is the last European whose beauty is not solely a pretense, a false allure.

The scene of *The Wings of the Dove* is the western world: the New York home of Milly Theale [14] and the London and Venice settings embrace the moral as well as the geographical limits of western culture. The England which has its center in Lancaster Gate (ironically the entrance to the English past leads but to hideous modernity) is given over completely to materialism. Its art has degenerated to the colossal vulgarity of Maud Lowder, the "Britannia of the Market Place" (XIX, 30) in whom "There was a whole side of Britannia, the side of her florid philistinism, her plumes and her train, her fantastic furniture and heaving bosom, the false gods of her taste and false notes of her talk . . ." (XIX, 31). The England of Maud Lowder has found the aristocratic

legacy of manners at odds with the material drive, and has thus
drained it of content. Force it finds more effective. Imperial and
gross, Maud is a lioness; she is imagined as outfitted with "a hel-
met, a shield, a trident and a ledger" (XIX, 31). The emblematic
Maud is blind to all but mass and quantity. She is "the most remarkable woman in England" (XIX, 180) because she sets the
tone for an empire, because she is "unscrupulous and immoral"
(XIX, 31) in an absolute way. The lesser figures about her,
Lord Mark and Lionel Croy, are less typical only in that they are
less effective. Maud Lowder's London is essentially the same as
the London of *What Maisie Knew* and *The Awkward Age*, with
the major difference that in *The Wings* James has made it unmistakably clear that the part stands for the whole.

Money is the controlling force in *The Wings of the Dove;* in
the London world the economic drive is the normal motivation.
Milly recognizes early that her English friends "appeared all . . .
to think tremendously of money" (XIX, 195). Economic values
subvert human values throughout, not just in Kate's identification
of Milly with her wealth, the easy assumption that leads to the
central action of the novel, but in the systematic reduction of all
quality to quantity. For example, Kate's father and sister reject
Kate's offer of family loyalty in favor of her potential cash value
as Aunt Maud's ward. Aunt Maud visualizes Kate as a financial
hold: ". . . I've been keeping [Kate's presence] for the comfort
of my declining years. I've watched it long; I've been saving it up
and letting it, as you say of investments, appreciate, and you may
judge whether, now it has begun to pay so, I'm likely to consent
to treat for it with any but a high bidder" (XIX, 82). Milly to
Maud also has negotiable value, as a bribe to Densher: "The
pieces fell together for him as he felt her thus buying him off, and
buying him . . . with Miss Theale's money" (XX, 67). The relationship between Kate and Densher gradually becomes corrupted through association with the acquisitive drive; the natural
has been made unnatural, so much so that Kate's visit to Densher's rooms is thought of by both as a payment for services rendered. Densher fondly thinks of "The force of the engagement,
the quantity of the article to be supplied, the special solidity of the
contract, the way, above all, as a service for which the price

named by him had been magnificently paid . . ." (XX, 237). Kate, before she formulates her plan, predicts that "Milly would pay a hundred per cent—and even to the end, doubtless, through the nose . . . (XIX, 180)." Milly, though she is morally detached from her wealth and innocent in spite of her millions, dies a victim of economic competition.[15]

It is particularly significant that Milly's great deed consists of a bestowal of her money. It is an act of love, an expression of forgiveness, and a transcendence of self. Nevertheless, since money is the destructive force in the novel, the nature of the act is tainted, although its motive is not. Milly's benevolence cannot purify her money. It is appropriate that the practical result of her gift is to sever Kate and Densher, for it was a want of money that kept them from marrying in the beginning. Milly is not corrupted by her money; yet the possession of it causes her destruction. Money destroys those who are associated with it—those who have it, those who desire it, those who contend for it.

Thus, one's moral stature is determined by the degree to which he is free from money. Maud Lowder is surely damned from the beginning; and Kate demonstrates her own damnation at the end, when she rejects spirit for matter, when she burns the unread letter of grace but rips open the envelope containing the check. In giving her the money, Densher gives "poor Kate her freedom" (XX, 396): the ambiguity of her being poor spiritually when rich materially and enslaved morally when free economically points the hard lesson of James's novel. Milly grows dependent on money only when social pressures compel her to buy the sanctuary of Palazzo Leporelli and the protection of Eugenio. She uses her wealth as "a counter-move to fate" (XX, 142). Yet she gains her lasting salvation only when she renounces money utterly.

Money and manners conflict throughout. In a society in which the only reality is money, traditional forms of intercourse—which should ideally reflect honor, sincerity, and intelligence—are necessarily false and hollow; and yet they constitute the last barrier against barbarism. The ambiguity of manners in *The Wings of the Dove* is well conveyed when Milly confronts Densher, just returned from his American tour, and Kate in the National Gallery. Having been suspicious all along of Kate's closeness to Densher and continually embarrassed by Kate's concealment of the intimacy, Milly is placed in the false position of having to pretend surprise at the discovery of their attachment. Kate and Densher are discomfited also; yet they too must carry on the pretense. The weight of the unspoken—the real—oppresses Milly. She sadly recognizes that the incident obviates any closeness in her future dealings with Kate and Densher. Yet, without the elaborate pretense that all is just as it should be—with the jointly maintained lie that Densher's visit to the United States is an appropriate conversation piece—the entire situation would collapse: all would be exposed and isolation would be total. If manners, what Densher calls "The mere aesthetic instinct of mankind" (XX, 299), are strained and deceptive, they yet remain necessary for social existence.

For Maud and Kate manners are the machinery for economic gain; for Densher and Milly they prohibit sincerity and intensity in personal relationships. Milly and Densher are among the first of James's protagonists to seek beauty and truth not in human institutions, now sterile and meaningless, but in human nature itself. James's approach is the same in *The Wings of the Dove;* he can define neither good nor evil in terms of national or social contexts. Milly's capacity for good is not so much a native American trait as it is a purely spiritual, literally a supernatural, power. Evil springs not from a rotten aristocracy, as in *The American,* or from the abandonment of national innocence, as in *The Portrait of a Lady,* but quite simply from human nature. Taken singly, the "villains" of *The Wings* have nothing of the absolute malignity that James finds in persons like Gilbert Osmond, who is ego-driven to an absolute degree and ruthless in his tyranny. Nothing of the same can be said of the malefactors in *The Wings,* whose actions or inactions are caused by common human failings: Aunt Maud is driven by social ambition, Kate by the need to rise above her unfortunate circumstances, Densher by weakness of will, and Lord Mark by stupidity and spite.

Evil in *The Wings* is the evil of the normal, and yet it produces such a monstrous catastrophe that the imbalance between suggested cause and obvious effect is extreme. James implies that though evil exists only in human relationships, it does not origi-

nate entirely in man's will; it is in the very scheme of things.[16] The
intrigue against Milly is planned by Kate, but the plot derives
ultimately from circumstances beyond the control of any of the
characters. Stephen Spender has said of James's last novels that
they contain no villains, that the situation is the villain.[17] This is
largely true, even though James, neither a determinist nor a
fatalist, holds his agents of evil morally responsible for their
crimes.

The ancestral curse is James's metaphor for the evil in the
world beyond the power of the human will. Both Milly and Kate,
we are told, are destined to suffer for the sins of their ancestors,
Milly by dying early and Kate by committing a great sin. Milly's
family has been plagued by a long history of early deaths and
widespread disaster. Kate also partakes mysteriously in the failure and disaster that have visited all her relatives and ancestors.
Early in the story, Kate thinks of her family: "Why should a set
of people have been put in motion, on such a scale and with such
an air of being equipped for a profitable journey, only to break
down without an accident, to stretch themselves in the wayside
dust without a reason?" (XIX, 4). Here James suggests the
capriciousness of fate, the inevitability of failure and unhappiness.
In *The Wings of the Dove* James associates the destinies of his
characters with a specific world-view more explicitly than in any
other novel. He suggests, if not the intervention of malign gods,
at least the prevalence of a law of life which cripples the deserv-
ing from the start.

While Milly is foredoomed to be a victim of evil, Kate is foredoomed to be an agent of evil. She shares mysteriously in the
unnamed crime of her father. She tells Densher that her father's
crime is "a part of me" (XIX, 68). The suggestions of ancestral
guilt and hereditary predestination are slight in *The Wings of the
Dove*, but they are significant; they support James's stress on the
general malignity of fallen human nature, rather than the evil of
particular villains.

Milly Theale's death is the effect of both illness and betrayal;
eventually physical and emotional pain become indistinguishable.
The point is that through Milly, James shows the relationship
between Kate's crime and the common frailty of man. The

inevitable and the calculated merge to kill Milly. Milly draws universal meaning from her illness: she identifies her doomed state with that of mankind. In his preface James speaks of "the communities of doom" [18] which surround Milly; to Milly everyone is in a "community of collapse with her" (XIX, 290). When she leaves Sir Luke's office knowing that she is fated to an early death, she projects her despair into the world about her. Milly wanders through the grimiest section of London and identifies herself with the children she sees playing:

> Here were benches and smutty sheep; here were idle lads at games of ball, with their cries mild in the thick air; here were wanderers anxious and tired like herself; here doubtless were hundreds of others just in the same box. Their box, their great common anxiety, what was it, in this grim breathing-space, but the practical question of life? (XIX, 250).

Milly's sense of the menacing relates the attitudes and actions of Kate, Densher, and Aunt Maud—each of whom represents a different kind of human weakness—to the general human fate.

When the civilized community falls apart James and his intelligent characters must transcend the temporal and the local to try to understand experience in terms of unchanging human nature and the permanent conditions of life. Kate, Milly, and Densher reach the point where they can no longer exist as morally free creatures in terms of manners or money, and therefore must acknowledge or renounce their humanity. Since society is dehumanized, to be human is to be socially isolated. Only through morality—and not through manners or money—can humanity be achieved.

Milly Theale's assumption that her siege of London will mean full nourishment of the sensibilities is an ironic illusion. She soon recognizes that her celebrated "success" is cheap and false. The great world, or the great English world, has simply crumpled beneath the weight of materialism. Unlike Strether and Maggie Verver, she recognizes rapidly that the old forms of civilization are empty. Soon after leaving her Alpine peak and plunging into the "abyss" [19] of the London world, she finds "society," in the sense of traditional and splendid styles of conduct, to be superficial and pretentious. Lord Mark's surface is soon penetrated: "Why did he hover before her as a potentially insolent noble? . . . she had, on the spot, with her first plunge into the obscure depths of a society constituted from far back, encountered the interesting phenomenon of complicated, of possibly sinister motive" (XIX, 152–154). Milly's "banquet of initiation" in London society is primarily an introduction to the false, substanceless manners that thinly disguise the greed beneath. Even in the early London chapters we look forward to Densher's wry reflection on the world he finds himself in: "He had supposed himself civilised; but if this was civilisation——! One could smoke one's pipe outside when twaddle was within" (XX, 44). Or we may look forward to the central image of a later James novel, the cracked crystal bowl gilded in gold.

Cut off in the beginning from any real relation with "all the ages" (XIX, 109), Milly seeks meaning in art. She finds "largeness of style" (XIX, 208) not at Lancaster Gate but at Matcham, and not through society but art. Milly leaves the Alps for London because "it had rolled over her that what she wanted of Europe was 'people' . . ." (XIX, 134). In the overstuffed vulgarity of Lancaster Gate, however, the reality of egotism is unrelieved and virtually undisguised by the appearance of art. But at Matcham people and scene merge into a single vision—a picture. "The great historic house had, for Milly, beyond terrace and garden, as the centre of an almost extravagantly grand Watteau-composition, a tone as of old gold kept 'down' by the quality of the air, summer full-flushed but attuned to the general perfect taste" (XIX, 208). Here life comes up to art—in a single splendid illusion for Milly: "Everything was great, of course, in great pictures, and it was doubtless precisely a part of the brilliant life—since the brilliant life, as one had faintly figured it, just *was* humanly led—that all impressions within its area partook of its brilliancy . . ." (XIX, 209). The "mild common carnival of good nature—a mass of London people together" (XIX, 218) gains immensely through the atmosphere of beauty, so that Milly unconsciously dismisses her earlier impressions of ugliness. If society were art, she thinks, then "to accept it without question might be as good a way as another of feeling life" (XIX, 219). The empty chatter of Lord

Mark and the banalities of people named Lord and Lady Alder-
shaw are transformed by the transcendent beauty of the Bronz-
ino. "Once more things melted together—the beauty and the history and the facility and the splendid midsummer glow: it was a
sort of magnificent maximum, the pink dawn of an apotheosis
coming so curiously soon" (XIX, 220). The apotheosis is personal
and prophetic, rather than social and actual; it suggests that only
through death and suffering can Milly approach the magnificence
of art, that, according to a basic metaphor of the novel, Milly can
go up only by going down, that she can be reborn into the im-
mortal beauty of the portrayed woman only by being, like her,
"dead, dead, dead" (XIX, 221).

But until her apotheosis art and life remain the separate poles of
Milly's experience. There are several efforts at reconciliation,
with results always tenuous and implications always ironic. In the
National Gallery, Milly finds refuge from an English society that
Kate had but shortly before described to her as "a strange and
dreadful monster, calculated to devour the unwary, to abase the
proud, to scandalize the good . . ." (XIX, 277). The relief af-
forded by "the quiet chambers, nobly overwhelming, rich but
slightly veiled" (XIX, 287–288), clashes startlingly with the
revelation of the real. The scene parallels the recognition scene in
The Ambassadors, when Strether's imaginative Lambinet—Europe as art—fuses with his vision of evil—Europe as life. A tourist's oblique observation that what she sees is "In the English
style" (XIX, 291) at first is taken by Milly to be a reference to a
painting, but she soon sees that the subject of the comment is
Merton Densher. Life intrudes upon art, and unlike the situation
in *The Ambassadors*, in which a synthesis occurs, here there is
only clash. The relief of the gallery gives way to the pain of social existence.

Beginning with Book Sixth the strain of maintaining appearances drives Milly to art—to her rented Venetian palace, which is
inadequate because its beauty, its inherent traditional values, its
silent profundity reflect nothing of the Europe of the early twentieth century. James dramatizes throughout the second volume
the meaning of Venice in the modern world: it, like London, has
made the sacrifice of art to matter (James may be invoking the

commercial as well as the aesthetic past of the Italian city), so that
Palazzo Leporelli has the same relation to the controlling ethos of
Venice as does Matcham to that of London. "Palazzo Leporelli
held its history still in its great lap, even like a painted idol, a solemn puppet hung about with decorations" (XX, 135). The
imagery suggests artificiality and sterility, for the essential Venice is better represented by the shady commercialism of Eugenio
and Pasquale. Although granted a luster by Susan Stringham's
journalistic imagination and by Milly's presence, the old palace
along the Grand Canal is but a relic of a decayed past.[20]

The Venetian past is purposefully present not in its beauty,
but in its evil—the two components of Europe that formed an
inseparable unity to the earlier James. Densher, the man of intellect, sees the Venetians of the present as "members of a race in
whom vacancy was but a nest of darknesses—not a vain surface,
but a place of withdrawal in which something obscure, something always ominous, indistinguishably lived" (XX, 256). When
Lord Mark awakens Milly to the monstrous plot against her, the
Venetian scene reflects the personal catastrophe and gives it extensive dimensions. The great black storm means tumult and
cataclysm. "It was a Venice all of evil that had broken out . . . a
Venice of cold lashing rain from a low black sky, of wicked wind
raging through narrow passes, of general arrest and interruption
. . ." (XX, 259). The Piazza San Marco, symbolic of European
civilization as a whole, is darkened to blackness and overwhelmed
by violence: "the whole place, in its huge elegance, the grace of
its conception and the beauty of its detail, was more than ever like
a great drawing-room, the drawing-room of Europe, profaned
and bewildered by some reverse of fortune" (XX, 261). The
effort of all to contain evil by appearances fails. Milly Theale's
death is the death of a civilization: the grey of a London dominated by materialism and the black of a Venice traditionally malign combine to kill her.

Milly believes that she can resist pain only by remaining in the
fortress tower of her palace, surrounded by the sterile formali-
ties of art. "Ah not to go down—never, never to go down" (XX,
147), she sighs to the uncomprehending Lord Mark. The idea of
"remaining aloft in the divine dustless air" (XX, 147) is a false

approach to the ideal, for purification and apotheosis require for James, as for Conrad, immersion in the destructive element. Thus when Milly does "come down" (XX, 203), literally to "the great saloon" (XX, 203) beneath her rooms in Palazzo Leporelli, figuratively to the abyss of human life, she discards for the first time "her almost monastic, her hitherto inveterate black" (XX, 214), the color of death, for white, the color of life. The incident is a picture: Milly diffusing "in wide warm waves the spell of a general, a kind of beatific mildness" (XX, 213); Densher and Kate speaking, for the first time, of the unspeakable—"Since she's to die I'm to marry her?" (XX, 225). Just as the historic grandeur of Matcham has transformed the ugly into the beautiful, so the splendor of the descent of the dove brings to the scene of betrayal the enveloping atmosphere of art. For once Susan Stringham's extravagant imagination has validity: "It's a Veronese picture, as near as can be . . ." (XX, 206), she tells Densher. But unlike her tower, Milly's surroundings below have human composition. "You're in the picture" (XX, 207), Kate tells Densher, and so is everyone. Life and art fuse when Milly goes down: ". . . Milly, let loose among them in a wonderful white dress, brought them somehow into relation with something that made them more finely genial; so that if the Veronese picture of which he had talked with Mrs. Stringham was not quite constituted, the comparative prose of the previous hours, the traces of insensibility qualified by 'beating down,' were at last almost nobly disowned" (XX, 213). Surrounded by her conspirators, the white-robed Milly begins to live just as she begins to die. "Since I've lived all these years as if I were dead, I shall die, no doubt, as if I were alive . . ." (XIX, 199), she had said earlier. It is then not the art of the gallery or of the palace that will enable Milly "to live," but the moral response to immoral humanity, which becomes in itself spiritual beauty.

Through Milly's developing awareness of the irrelevance of the art of the past to modern life, James dramatizes the disintegration of civilization. Throughout the novel he reveals the ever widening breach between individual needs and the social framework. One inevitably finds himself in a position where he must define himself through either his social position or his isolated self. De-

prived of access to meaning through art or manners, Maud
Lowder derives her motivations and morality from British culture
in general. We find her in the beginning as we find her in the end
—a loyal apostle to money. But Kate, Densher, and Milly are, in
the beginning, undefined by status or creed. The novel records
their efforts and decisions toward achieving identity. For each the
existing situation is inadequate.

Kate's personal qualities are great: she esteems family loyalty
over private gain, the need for love over the need for profit, and
moral freedom over moral commitment. But her father, her sister,
and her aunt comprise for her a world in which selfhood and
vulgarity set the tone, in which the material urge is unrefined by
sentiment or sensibility. Thus, in her visit to her father's squalid
rooms, we find Kate for the most part glancing into the mirror,
holding fast to that which is herself.

In Kate's case the standard Jamesian ambiguity towards
money has an added twist. The ordinary dilemma is there: to
acquire money is ugly, but the possession of it is the *sine qua non*
for the good life. In most of James's novels, however, the social
scene itself remains aloof from the economic process: fortune-
hunter and business man alike are anomalies, inconsistent with
the placid solemnity of age and beauty. But the London world
can be understood only in terms of money. To pursue magnificence Kate has no choice but to accept the code of Aunt Maud.
Her effort to reconcile the human value of love and the barbaric
value of money must fail. In her struggle to avoid Aunt Maud
and yet gain a fortune, she becomes an Aunt Maud herself. Therefore, when she seeks her own image in Densher's mirror in the
novel's final scene, she signalizes her separation from her lover,
whose own renunciation of money forces Kate to retreat to the
damning security of wealth.

Kate's initial conflict is between acceptance of family poverty
for the sake of loyalty and acceptance of Aunt Maud's wealth for
the sake of magnificence. When Kate, rebuffed by her father and
sister, moves to Lancaster Gate, she hesitates to surrender her
will to Maud. In "her actual high retreat" (XIX, 56–57) above
Maud's "counting-house" (XIX, 30), she is precariously detached
and uncommitted. The parallel to Milly in her tower is clear

enough. Here Kate's relation to Maud forecasts Milly's eventual
relation to Kate. But when Kate descends she reconciles the
standards of Maud with her love for Densher, and thus becomes
converted to society; whereas Milly holds firm to her personal
values, her moral integrity.

What we find in Kate is a great will that accepts and then uses
society on its own terms. Her object is money and her method is
manners. Once she initiates her plot, from the moment she decides not to tell Milly about her engagement to Densher, she
remains inflexible. To Densher, Kate is "deep" (XIX, 175), "a
whole library of the unknown, the uncut" (XX, 62), but ironically there is nothing beneath the surface but the will: the moral
intelligence has surrendered itself to money.

To the very end Densher marvels at Kate's "high sobriety and
her beautiful self-command. . . . she had her perfect manner,
which *was* her decorum" (XX, 316). Because of her mastery
over manners, her skillful control of appearances, her intrigue
almost succeeds. But the lady of appearances pays the great price
of being definable only through appearances; she is magnificent
only in contrast with the cheap and the showy. In Venice Kate's
brilliance pales before Milly's: "As a striking young presence she
was practically superseded . . ." (XX, 216). Later, when Densher meets Kate at Marion's wretched house, he observes that
"Kate wouldn't have been in the least the creature she was if
what was just round them hadn't mismatched her . . ." (XX,
365). The conclusion of course reveals Kate's magnificence for
what it is—a thing of death—in contrast with the life-giving
spiritual magnificence of Milly.

If Kate commits herself to Aunt Maud, Densher commits himself to Kate. But his association always admits the possibility of
his detachment. For one thing, Densher becomes involved not
through strength of will, but through weakness of will; for another, his motivation is not greed, but love. His loyalty to Kate,
like Kate's loyalty to Maud, is an imperfect moral standard, but
it is supported by affection rather than a prudent concern for
appearances.

Densher too at the beginning is uncommitted. His James-like
continental education has given him, if not a moral firmness, at

least a detachment from the English trait of regarding money
excessively. In his quest for identity, Densher—through Milly's
grace—choses the hitherto unrealized self over the materialism
of his age. Through indecision he becomes implicated in Kate's
scheme. His good nature and gentlemanliness carry him through
to deceive Milly. But when he finds the demands of appearance
too oppressive, he finds the necessity of self-assertion compelling.
In his brooding walks about Venice, Densher faces fully "the
interesting question of whether he had really no will left" (XX,
177). His problem is really very much the same as Milly's, for,
unlike Maud and Kate, both require the sustenance of immediate
and honest personal relationships, which are by definition un-
attainable in a society held together by appearances. Since the
association with Kate has been beclouded by duplicity, he seeks
out—half-consciously—the companionship of Milly. Densher's
passion and Milly's love are both frustrated by Kate's scheme of
appearances.

Densher is a forerunner of a dominant character type of modern literature: he leads to Eliot's Prufrock, Conrad's Heyst, and
Greene's Scobie. He is the nonheroic yet perceptive man, driven
to self-understanding by his weakness of will and horror of
ugliness. Like Kate and Milly, Densher plunges into the abyss,
which for him as for the others is both internal and external—
the private depths and the social depths. If Milly's descent to the
abyss reveals spiritual love and Kate's reveals only will, Densher's reveals, not the will he had sought to find, but a capacity
for sanctifying grace. For he remains weak always. His suffering
is most acute when he is isolated—after his moral rejection of
Kate, but before his acceptance of Milly's love. When Sir Luke
leaves the dying Milly to Densher alone, the physician's unspoken
plea that he love Milly leads Densher to ask himself "into what
abyss it pushed him . . ." (XX, 309). Densher soars from the
abyss, too late to save Milly, but not too late to be saved by her;
he embraces spirit over flesh.

In a world whose institutional and aesthetic heritage has been
drained of moral meaning, there can be no ultimately valid
achievement for the James character without "the final authority
of selfhood." [21] Thus the romantic epithets that Susan Stringham

applies to Milly Theale lack real significance: the heiress of all
the ages has an inheritance of corruption only; the princess reigns
in a morally bankrupt empire. But Kate and, for the most part,
Densher also miss the point by being too prosaic about Milly. To
Kate, Milly is identified primarily with her fortune; to Densher
she is the "little American girl" (XX, 174). Milly's descent to the
abyss precedes the apotheosis of the dove—her transfigured self.
Milly can acquire identity only by assaulting life, by risking
everything. And not until her great and lonely moral achievement does Milly assume an identity independent of the social,
economic, and aesthetic structures which had previously estab-
lished, for others and for herself, her reality and her being.

The Golden Bowl

In *The Golden Bowl* James achieves a resolution of the Eu-
rope-America antithesis principally because he is hesitant to
place the burden of evil on the Europeans. It is the human
situation itself which produces the intense moral evil of the
novel, rather than the deeds of particular characters or sets of
characters. In *The Golden Bowl* James continues to dramatize
the moral, cultural, and temperamental differences between the
American and the European, but he reveals that the common
denominator of the two is their mutual participation in human sin.

The problem of *The Golden Bowl* is easily formulated, for it is
contained in the central symbolism of the bowl itself. The Golden
Bowl stands mainly for Maggie Verver's marriage. The bowl
contains a flaw, which stands for the defect in the marriage. To
define the flaw is to define the evil of the situation.

It is a gross oversimplification to assume that the only evil is
the adulterous tie between Prince Amerigo and Charlotte Stant.
James stresses the equally grave, though less sensational, moral
defects in the wealthy American art collector and his daughter.
In *The Golden Bowl* James takes American innocence less at face
value than in any previous work; he dispassionately analyzes the
serious moral shortcomings of the Ververs. He neither judges
them nor implies that they are better or worse than the Europeans, but he dramatizes their role in the creation of the flaw in
the golden bowl. The adultery is the objectification of the evil,

the prime dramatic act of evil; but behind the actual adultery is a complex of motives and attitudes which leads inexorably to the relatively simple matter of unfaithfulness and comprises the essential evil.

Because of the way the story is told, James's criticism of the Ververs remains implicit rather than explicit. The first half of the novel comes from the point of view of the Prince, whose gentleness and urbanity prevent him from thinking of his wife and father-in-law as anything other than kind and just. Maggie, the center of consciousness in the second half of the novel, rarely realizes her own shortcomings. Fanny Assingham, who provides several illuminating comments about the Prince and Charlotte, seems unaware of the Ververs' flaws—even though some of her general observations are ironically applicable to them—and thus she, the only confidante of the novel, cannot function as a consistently judicious and perceptive chorus.

Nevertheless, through dialogue, action, and imagery, James reveals his attitude toward the Ververs.[22] Their faults stem mainly from their innocence and their power. Both Maggie and Mr. Verver are naïve and simple, incapable of understanding their own lives and those of others. Thus, particularly in the case of Mr. Verver, James describes them as children. Instead of realizing that they are involved in adult marriages, the American father and daughter act as if they are playing games: "They were fairly at times, the dear things, like children playing at paying visits, playing at 'Mr. Thompson and Mrs. Fane,' each hoping that the other would really stay to tea" (XXIII, 252). Often Mr. Verver gives the impression of "handling a relic of infancy—sticking on the head of a broken soldier or trying the lock of a wooden gun" (XXIII, 126–127). The Ververs are "good children, bless their hearts, and the children of good children; so that verily the Principino himself, as less consistently of that descent, might figure to the fancy as the ripest genius of the trio" (XXIII, 334).

The infant king and the princess play the game of living as adults. The fairyland in which they live, however, is the real world: Mr. Verver is the king of a great empire; Maggie, unlike Milly Theale, is a real princess. James does not divest American innocence of its moral sense, but he exposes its ignorance and its

inclination to romanticize life. Fanny Assingham, in one of her
most clear-sighted observations, remarks that "stupidity pushed
to a certain point *is*, you know, immorality. Just so what is morality but high intelligence?" (XXIII, 88). Fanny, in her utilitarian
and merely social conception of morality, is ignorant of the implications of her statement and of its application to the Ververs;
nevertheless the outcome of their marriages proves her right.

Unlike most American innocents, the Ververs are not taken
advantage of because of their ignorance of evil; rather they help
create evil because of their ignorance. Curiously the Ververs'
ignorance is hardly distinguishable from their selfishness. They
are unconcerned with the Prince and Charlotte as persons, for
they are unaware of life outside of themselves and they know
nothing of the meaning of marriage.

Early in the story, even before his marriage, Prince Amerigo
thinks of Americans as "incredibly romantic" (XXIII, 11). Maggie's romanticism is a blend of ignorance, optimism, and senti-
mentality. The Prince says to her, "You see too much—that's
what may sometimes make you difficulties. When you don't at
least . . . see too little" (XXIII, 11). If Maggie sees too much,
she sees too much of herself in others; she is eventually betrayed
by her belief that the Prince can be expected to fit comfortably
in the little niche which she has arranged for him. If she sees too
little, it is the existence of evil—actual and potential—to which
she is blinded. The Prince soon notes Maggie's inclination to shy
away from any significant (adult) questions:

> He had perceived on the spot that any *serious* discussion of
> veracity, of loyalty, or rather of the want of them, practically
> took her unprepared, as if it were quite new to her. He had
> noticed it before: it was the English, the American sign that
> duplicity, like "love," had to be joked about. It couldn't be
> "gone into" (XXIII, 15).

Fanny Assingham idealizes Maggie consistently. She tells her
husband that Maggie "wasn't born to know evil. She must never
know it" (XXIII, 78). Undoubtedly James thinks otherwise. He
accepts neither Fanny's estimate of Maggie nor Maggie's estimate
of herself. He ironically contrasts Maggie's sentiments and words

with her actions, showing that in spite of her optimism and goodness she is a contributor to evil. Maggie's ignorance shields her
from guilt, even though it is because of her ignorance, added to
the power of her wealth, that she is an agent of evil. Maggie
blandly buys herself a prince, then neglects him to be with her
father, and realizes only fitfully her part in undermining her own
happiness.

It is ironic that idealism motivates the "purchases" of the
Ververs. They are not American robber barons in the ordinary
sense; they supplement the acquisitiveness of the American com-
mercialist with a kind of high idealism, unconcerned with simple
profit. Mr. Verver's explicit reason for being in Europe is to stock
an art museum which he has constructed for the edification of the
citizens of "American City." Maggie and her father have much to
say about their unselfishness, but basically they are unselfish only
to each other and exhibit their mutual altruism at the expense of
others, most notably the Prince and Charlotte. Maggie marries
the Prince as a favor to her father: to enrich his personal collection, to free him from the care of her. Mr. Verver, through selfless devotion to his daughter, marries Charlotte. Maggie had suggested his marriage originally; the elder Verver agrees in order to
satisfy her, all the while unconcerned about the nature of marriage
and his duty toward Charlotte.

The trouble with the Ververs' transcendental idealism is that it
is too much removed from ordinary life. The section of the novel
which describes Mr. Verver's proposal to Charlotte conveys the
limitations and shallowness of that idealism. First it is notable
that Mr. Verver suggests that Charlotte accompany him to Brighton, where he plans to purchase a set of rare tiles. The association
of Charlotte with the purchase of the tiles has an obvious symbolic value, which is increased and deepened with the visit to the
owner of the pieces. He is a poor man, burdened by a large family; yet within the house there beats the "pulse of life" (XXIII,
211). Mr. Verver is oblivious of the humanity of the scene.
Furthermore, the Brighton scene is not a golden one: it is un-
embellished by art or money. James dramatizes Mr. Verver's
inability to deal with life realistically, by showing the disparity
between his childish romantic conceptions and unadorned reality.

In his proposal to Charlotte, Mr. Verver demonstrates this deficiency further. He is pathetically unresponsive to Charlotte's humor and vitality:

> It really came home to [him] on the spot that this free range of observation in her, picking out the frequent funny with extraordinary promptness, would verily henceforth make a different thing for him of such experiences, of the customary hunt for the valuable prize, the inquisitive play of his accepted monomania . . . (XXIII, 213).

Mr. Verver at first misrepresents his intentions to Charlotte; he tells her that he wishes simply to be kind to her. But Charlotte, not a deceptive adventuress by any means, spots the weakness of his argument and calls his attention to the disparity between his avowed concern for herself and his obviously deeper love for Maggie: "She's everything to you—she has always been. Are you so certain that there's room in your life—?" Mr. Verver can lie no longer: "To put her at peace is . . . what I'm trying, with you, to do" (XXIII, 222–223).

Mr. Verver's ignorance, his acquisitiveness, his dependence on a lie—all for the sake of "his majestic scheme" (XXIII, 210), his "exciting, inspiring, uplifting" (XXIII, 208) idea—unquestionably place a burden of moral responsibility on him and reveal the insidious and hypocritical side of his magnanimity.

Both he and Maggie, however, are only objectively hypocritical. Neither wishes to deceive. There are many characters in James who bring about evil though they are unaware of its existence, but the Ververs are the only ones whose imperception is unconditioned by either self-interest or self-righteousness. Yet it is precisely James's point that a pure motive and straightforward conduct can lead to evil if the intelligence is deficient. To James a morality based on feeling is dangerous as well as sentimental; the only true morality originates in intelligence.

On the other hand, if the Ververs arrange their marriages with ignorance, the Prince and Charlotte are intelligent and prudent in carrying out their agreements. It is a piece of bad luck that through lack of funds the two lovers have been unable to marry. With maturity and decency they renounce their attachment to each other to marry into the Verver family. James stresses Amerigo's noble intentions prior to his marriage: "If there was one thing in the world the young man at this juncture clearly intended it was to be much more decent as a son-in-law than lots of fellows he could think of had shown themselves in the character" (XXIII, 5). The Prince is obviously disturbed by Charlotte's inopportune visit. Charlotte, however, does not come (at least not consciously) as a marriage-wrecker; she is convinced of her strength of purpose. Fanny Assingham, who is a reliable analyst of her two friends from Italy, believes in the good intentions of Charlotte: "She doesn't deliberately intend, she doesn't consciously wish, the least complication. It's perfectly true that she thinks Maggie a dear—as who doesn't? She's incapable of any *plan* to hurt a hair of her head" (XXIII, 70). Charlotte's hesitance to marry Mr. Verver, because of sincere reservations about his motives, shows her to be seeking neither a fortune nor easy access to the Prince.

Also Charlotte and the Prince combine good intentions with intelligence, while Maggie and her father combine them with ignorance. However, with the Prince and Charlotte good intentions go along with a deficiency of moral strength, so that the insulting treatment accorded them by their *sposi* makes their adultery inevitable. The Prince, as an Italian, and Charlotte, as a Europeanized American, lack the moral sense which the Ververs have in abundance. Early in the novel, Amerigo explains to Fanny Assingham, with acute self-knowledge, the delicate balance in his own nature between his lack of a firm moral foundation and his determination to remain irreproachable: "Of my real honest fear of being 'off' some day, of being wrong, *without* knowing it. That's what I shall always trust you for—to tell me when I am. No—with you people it's a sense. We haven't got it— not as you have" (XXIII, 30–31).

The Prince's latent immorality is hereditary. Amerigo is aware of a side of his nature that is independent of his background— his decency, his good intentions—and a side of his nature which is inherited—his refinement and culture, but also his ancestral guilt, his latent capacity for evil. It is ironic that the Ververs find him attractive as a relic of old Rome, even though the Prince often warns that his history is associated with violence and criminality, remotely with the crimes of the Borgias. It is, therefore, fitting that Maggie discovers ultimately in the Prince the fulfillment of his history which she had originally sought.

The Prince is associated with both his near and his remote past: he is a cultured gentleman, a man of the world. Charlotte, likewise, as an experienced and sophisticated traveller, with a rich past of her own, is associated indirectly but essentially with old Florence. Mrs. Assingham once compares her to a Borgia, alluding to her capacity for evil. Mr. Verver and Maggie habitually think of Charlotte as simply Maggie's playmate, and thus underestimate her as much as they do the Prince—though in a different way.

To complement their tastes and their temperaments, Amerigo and Charlotte require the large public life. The small and retiring Ververs, through a failure in intelligence, ignore these obvious needs; they thus not only provide the opportunity for the Prince and Charlotte to find in each other a means to happiness, but they also help cause such an illicit relationship. The mental unrest that precedes the Prince's actual sin points up again his superiority to the common adulterer. He is sincere and profound in his discontent; he is unable to interpret the Verver's neglect as a wrong against him. The affair begins not as a calculated act, but as an effect of boredom. The Prince is left alone at Portland Place while Maggie pays one of her regular visits to her father. Charlotte, who has left her own home out of a delicate sense of intrusion into the Verver's private life, comes to the Prince, seeking consolation and company. At first they discuss somberly and philosophically their mutual distress. The Prince ponders their curious arrangement; he concludes that "Nothing stranger surely had ever happened to a conscientious, a well-meaning, a perfectly passive pair: no more extraordinary decree had ever been launched against such victims than this of forcing them against their will into a relation of mutual close contact that they had done everything to avoid" (XXIII, 289).

James shows that a difference of personal and national traits causes evil. Moral and cultural differences isolate; they prevent social harmony. One of the cultural differences contributing to the evil in *The Golden Bowl* is between Charlotte's and Amerigo's conception of marriage, on the one hand, and Maggie's and Mr. Verver's, on the other. The spiritual love between father and daughter is not only different from but also inimical to the kind of physical love which Charlotte and the Prince ("The Prince's notion of a recompense to women . . . was more or less to make love to them" [XXIII, 21–22]) associate with marriage. As long as she is so close to her father, Maggie resists the Prince's sexuality. Amerigo desires "the maximum of immersion in the fact of being married" (XXIII, 148). Significantly it is Charlotte's sensuousness which tempts Amerigo: "He was occupied with Charlotte because in the first place she looked so inordinately handsome and held so high, where so much else was mature and sedate, the torch of responsive youth and the standard of passive grace . . ." (XXIII, 321).

In addition, the Prince maintains an ethical standard which he admits to be inferior to that of the Ververs: "it's always a question of doing the best for one's self one can—without injury to others" (XXIII, 58). Consistent with his creed, the Prince marries Maggie to gain for himself a large freedom, a contact with art and wealth, and a desirable social situation. On the other hand, he is satisfied that he is not taking unfair advantage of Maggie or acting from base motives. Charlotte, who also seeks freedom and position, responds similarly to Mr. Verver's proposal of marriage. Furthermore, the joint attitude of Charlotte and Amerigo need undergo no alteration or modification in order to permit an adultery between them. They agree that as long as they keep up appearances and act discreetly, they commit no crime. Thus, with the Prince and Charlotte, an absence of the American moral sense makes adultery possible. Both the Europeans and the Americans, then, have their faults, but it is the combination of European notions of ethics and American ignorance which produces the evil of the situation.

It is to the credit of Charlotte and the Prince that they have ties with Italy rather than with England. Like the Ververs they are on foreign soil in England. The England of *The Golden Bowl* is still the England of *What Maisie Knew*, of *The Awkward Age*, and of *The Wings of the Dove*. It is associated almost exclusively with middle-class materialism, with economic and social competi-

tion, with lust and greed, with irreverence and indignity, with a
decayed aristocracy. The Assinghams—Fanny with her genius
for social planning and the Colonel with his narrow economic
viewpoint—symbolize England. They also suggest the element
of greed and materialism that is present on all sides of the quad-
rangular marital arrangement of the Ververs. The Assinghams
reveal by contrast the moral superiority of the Ververs and of
the Prince and Charlotte, although at the same time they adum-
brate the flaws of each. Thus the high idealism of the Ververs
overshadows the Assinghams, but so does the integrity of Amerigo and Charlotte, whose consideration for their spouses, even
though limited, and whose ability to maintain dignity while committing adultery show their moral superiority to such English
adulterers as Maisie's parents. The Prince and Charlotte ennoble
what James treats most often as mere lust, so that their sin shares
somehow in the rich sensuousness of Renaissance Italy, to which
both have ties.

In spite of the many virtues of the adulterers, James reveals
their sins as well. R. P. Blackmur observes that "The act of illicit
love is the tragic fault . . . the act which can be explained but
which cannot be justified." [23] Adultery is always abhorrent to
James, and it remains so in *The Golden Bowl*, although here it is
equated not with willful betrayal or with animal lust, but with
universal human weakness. But since the illicit love occurs within
a marital arrangement—unlike the affairs in *The Ambassadors*
and *The Wings of the Dove*—it takes on a greater indecency
because of its perfidy. Mrs. Assingham and Maggie refer repeatedly to the affair as "lurid," "abominable," and "ugly" (XXIV,
127, 185, 111); unquestionably James's attitude toward it is the
same.

When Maggie learns of the affair, she does not consider it a
crime against herself. She sees it as a disarrangement of the perfect order she had visualized. Similarly James's attitude is that the
adultery is the most obvious deviation from the ideal order, contributing to the general flaw, which all four persons have helped
to create.

But the worst sin of the Prince and Charlotte is not adultery, but
deceit. As if to stress the seriousness of their deception, James

puts weight on their not disclosing to Maggie or her father their previous intimacy. Just as Kate and Densher betray Milly from the beginning by concealing their acquaintance with each other —a deception which leads easily and inevitably to their major deception—so it is the original insincerity of the Prince and Charlotte (whose mission with Amerigo to the gift shop is crucial) which portends the much graver deception that follows. Carl Van Doren writes that "For James, as for Maggie, the evil of the situation consisted less in the sin of adultery than in the ugliness of stealth and deceit." [24] Austin Warren concludes that "the great theme of *The Bowl* is the discovery that evil exists in the forms most disruptive to civilization: in disloyalty and treason." [25] In the second half of the novel, where the sense of evil is especially pervasive, Maggie is most horrified by deception.

Once their affair has begun, the Prince and Charlotte undergo a moral disintegration: they readily abandon the standards of honor and responsibility which had once sustained them. The Prince soon begins to rationalize his guilt, to place all the blame on the Ververs, to assume that because "he was . . . held cheap and made light of" (XXIII, 353), he is justified in his unfaithfulness. When Maggie, once conscious of Amerigo's defection, tries to regain his favor by attentiveness and consideration (in fact, by a deliberate appeal to his sensuality), he evades her; he wishes to maintain the existing arrangement. His intimacy with Charlotte has so affected him that he no longer wishes for Maggie to separate herself from her father. He now supports the evil he had previously condemned.

From the beginning Charlotte is morally unconscious. Her loyalty to Maggie and Mr. Verver restrains her from resuming her affair with the Prince. Once she falters, however, she subsides completely into sensuality. She loses concern for all but propriety; "We're happy—and they're happy" (XXIII, 341), she says. When the question of guilt arises, she blames either Fanny Assingham or, like the Prince, the Ververs.

James uses imagery of gold and golden objects to suggest a complex of motifs which underlies the main action. For example, there are recurrent references to the Golden Age. Mr. Verver

(Adam) and his daughter are often described in terms suggestive of an ideal pastoral state prior to the Fall of Man, especially in the scenes at Mr. Verver's country estate, Fawns. Fawns exists in "a wonderful windless waiting golden hour" (XXIII, 191), and is surrounded by "the general golden peace" (XXIII, 192). Everything at Fawns "with its uncorrected antiquity" is "conscious" of "no violence from the present and no menace from the future" (XXIV, 309). The association of the Ververs with a prelapsarian innocence has an ironic effect. The Ververs are not living in a golden age, but in a fallen world; and their conduct is motivated by a naïve belief in human perfection and, much worse, by the assumption that their "marriage" to each other stands as a normal, even an ideal, relationship. The Prince, who recognizes the absurdity of upholding the standards imposed on him by the Ververs, realizes that the Golden Age cannot be re-created, at least insofar as his relation with Charlotte is concerned.

> What was supremely grotesque in fact was the essential opposition of theories—as if a galantuomo, as *he* at least constitutionally conceived galantuomini, could do anything *but* blush to "go about" at such a rate with such a person as Mrs. Verver in a state of childlike innocence, the state of our primitive parents before the Fall (XXIII, 335).

The extreme innocence of the Ververs amounts to a kind of evil in itself; their ignorance of sin helps to cause a sin. Appropriately James describes the Verver's developing knowledge of evil also in terms of the dissolution of the golden atmosphere. When Maggie first suspects the defection of the Prince, she is forced to pay "tribute . . . to realities looming through the golden mist that had already begun to be scattered. The conditions facing her had yielded for the time to the golden mist—had considerably melted away . . ." (XXIV, 31).

An additional implication of the gold imagery is the suggestion of a contest of power between the old gold of Roman culture and the new gold of American wealth. As Francis Fergusson has stated, "the novel is a struggle for power. The power in question is, literally and in the beginning, that of Adam Verver's vast wealth; and the question is, who shall control it, and to what end?" [26] But the Prince possesses a power of his own, notably that of the ancient Roman Empire, transfigured and enhanced by Renaissance culture and art. Thus the new gold of Mr. Verver attracts and eventually absorbs the old gold of Amerigo. The Americans acquire European elegance and experience; the Europeans acquire American wealth. The Ververs initially refuse to accept the implications of a personal union with Europe, but Amerigo is fully conscious of the significance of his marriage. He sees himself becoming engulfed by a tide of new wealth: his early dealings with Maggie

> had but sweetened the waters in which he now floated, tinted them as by the action of some essence, poured from a gold-topped phial, for making one's bath aromatic. No one before him, never—not even the infamous Pope—had so sat up to his neck in such a bath. It showed for that matter how little one of his race could escape after all from history. What was it but history, and of *their* kind very much, to have the assurance of the enjoyment of more money than the palace-builder himself could have dreamed of? (XXIII, 10).

Maggie's synthesis of her own innocence and Amerigo's experience (each a blend of good and evil) dramatizes the struggle for power and status between the two great worlds. What Fergusson calls "the historic dimension of the novel" [27] is reflected in the personal conflict between the Europeans and the Americans. *The Golden Bowl* is basically a novel of the private life; yet the suggestion that the conflict is emblematic of a larger struggle between empires contributes a related theme. The evil that taints the Verver family likewise taints the historical movement of western civilization from Europe to America. James's point is that an assimilation between American wealth and European tradition cannot come about without a mutual contamination, without European experience in evil, in deceit, in treachery subverting American innocence. The common meeting ground of London stresses the materialism detrimental to an honorable union between Europe and America. Fanny Assingham is much worse than any of the major participants, but her opportunism, her concern for position, her readiness to lie and betray have their counterparts in Adam and Maggie Verver and in the Prince and Charlotte.

British materialism provides a particularly apt background to the novel: it reveals the baseness of the monetary struggle and counteracts the emphasis on the exotic and the golden, on the ancestral and aesthetic connotations of the same wealth that Colonel Assingham values only in terms of pounds and shillings. Naked greed motivates each of the marriage partners: the Ververs "buy" their *sposi;* Amerigo and Charlotte marry mainly because of the Verver fortune. R. W. Short writes that the most pervasive images in *The Golden Bowl* are those of "travel and machinery and 'ownership' (*money* or *property*). If these . . . do not alone set the tone, they create the story, inasmuch as it is the story of ever-moving homeless persons, trapped by the rarefied rigidities of society, all in some sense buying and selling each other." [28] Though not so much as *The Wings of the Dove, The Golden Bowl* is dominated by a drive for wealth and power that is disguised rather than transformed by the heavy golden atmosphere. James is not unaware that gold is also suggestive of money as loot, as unadorned wealth. The novel begins when the Prince, glancing at a London shop window, evaluates the assorted riches as ill-gotten, as sordid, and as representative of nothing more than plunder.

> He had strayed simply enough into Bond Street, where his imagination, working at comparatively short range, caused him now and then to stop before a window in which objects massive and lumpish, in silver and gold, in the forms to which precious stones contribute, or in leather, steel, brass, applied to a hundred uses and abuses, were as tumbled together as if, in the insolence of the Empire, they had been the loot of far-off victories (XXIII, 3).

The Golden Bowl stands for Maggie's marriage, but it is also a focal symbol of luxury and wealth. The gold of the bowl is the combined gold of the Ververs and of the Prince—new and old, American and European. The flashy exterior is, in both cases, misleading, for underneath is the cracked crystal, the evil center.

   If the dimensions of evil in *The Golden Bowl* are conveyed
through image motifs, the terror of Maggie Verver suggests the
force of the evil. In handling Maggie's awakening vision of evil,
James indicates that her suffering is not the gratuitous agony of
Lambert Strether, but in many ways a just punishment for her sin.
Maggie's sin is close in nature though not in gravity to that of
Gilbert Osmond. She recognizes that she and her father "liked to
think they had given their life this unusual extension and this
liberal form, which many families, many couples, and still more
pairs of couples, wouldn't have found workable" (XXIV, 5–6).
Maggie's *hybris* consists in her view of marriage as an extension
of herself. It is fitting that her suffering should consist in a dimin-
ishing of herself, in a severing from society, in a limiting of her
relationships with life. For Maggie suffers not so much from the
shock that follows knowledge as from the isolation that knowledge necessitates. She is isolated first of all from the Prince and
Charlotte inasmuch as she cannot allow them to know that she
knows without permanently destroying her marriage. What pains
Maggie most is her isolation from her father: "I must do everything . . . without letting papa see what I do—at least till it's
done" (XXIV, 38).

   The second volume of *The Golden Bowl* begins, insofar as
Maggie's experience with Europe is concerned, at that point
where *The Portrait of a Lady* ends—when the heroine realizes
that she has been betrayed. Significantly a greater sense of evil
emerges from the second than from the first half of the book.
Once Maggie learns of the initial evil, she tries to restore good to
the situation, or, in her own terms, to have the bowl "as it *was*
to have been. . . . The bowl without the crack" (XXIV, 216–
217). It is in the process of recovery that each member of the
circle is most oppressed by evil. Though Maggie is successful in
patching up the pieces of her smashed happiness, the darkness
that attends the restoration prevents *The Golden Bowl* from being anything but a somber novel.

   Once the point of view switches to Maggie, once she instead
of the Prince dominates the action, the sense of evil increases. One
reason is that Maggie more than anyone else suffers from the
joint crime of all. Her discovery of the adultery is her first vision

of evil, and her native sense of morality and fear of sexuality cause her to be more shocked and dismayed than a European would be.

Yet the full force of evil is not released until Maggie acts. Maggie's intervention augments the suffering of all. When a social situation is grounded in evil, all further behavior, even though motivated by high ideals and executed with intelligence, must intensify and partake of that evil. Maggie becomes deceiver, aggressor, and mistress of intrigue to gain her victory. Employing the techniques of the worldly-wise and practical-minded European, Maggie uses evil means to bring about a good end. No other means are available to her. To be candid would be to wreck the arrangement permanently and to alienate the Europeans. Maggie Verver reconciles American idealism and British practicality, combining, as it were, the spiritual love of Milly Theale and the practical genius of Kate Croy. James does not modify the ugliness of her intrigue, even though, in his ethical relativism, he reveals that moral motives may transcend and convert objectively immoral means.

Maggie's maneuver consists in aligning the Prince with her, thereby alienating him from Charlotte. To this end she bluntly tells the Prince that she knows of his affair. The Prince discovers a vitality in Maggie that previously he had found wanting. Therefore he rejects Charlotte; he refuses to tell her what Maggie knows. Maggie lies to Charlotte when she tells her that she suspects nothing. Maggie deceives her father also by not revealing her knowledge. Fanny Assingham, who also is compelled to lie— she pretends an innocence of the adultery so that Maggie may have a free hand in ending it—tells her husband, "We shall have . . . to lie for her—to lie till we're black in the face" (XXIV, 122).

The lie represents the compromise of good with evil. The Ververs' domestic arrangement is so perverse that only perverse means can improve it. Further evil and suffering must follow; and complete goodness and happiness can never be achieved. Certainly Maggie's solution is not an entirely satisfactory one. If there are gains there are also losses. A necessary loss is the severance of Maggie and her father, which, even though painful for both, is

of course required, for it was the unconscionable closeness of the
two which caused much of the initial evil. But there are gratuitous
losses as well. Charlotte Stant is sacrificed to the well-being of the
others. After her terrified anxiety over the deceit of Maggie and
the Prince, Charlotte's doom is completed when she is led off to a
sterile existence in America with Mr. Verver, who is described
as "holding in one of his pocketed hands the end of a long silken
halter looped round her beautiful neck" (XXIV, 287). Charlotte,
not Maggie, is the sacrificial victim, the scapegoat. Deprived of
her freedom, she is like a wounded beast, instinctive and impulsive
in her suffering as she has been in her happiness. Maggie has the
impression of "gilt wires and bruised wings, the spacious but
suspended cage, the home of eternal unrest, of pacings, beatings,
shakings all so vain, into which the baffled consciousness help-
lessly resolved itself. The cage was the deluded condition . . ."
(XXIV, 229). It may be an instance of poetic justice that Charlotte suffers the anguish of deception, because she has contributed
earlier to the deception of Maggie. But when the punishments
are meted out, there is no absolute justice. The Prince escapes
retribution, deprived only of a mistress whom he no longer loves.
At the conclusion, Charlotte, no more guilty than any of the
other three, is made to endure the most pain. As Maggie says, "It's
as if her unhappiness had been necessary to us—as if we had
needed her, at her own cost, to build us up and start us" (XXIV,
346). Charlotte is not only "doomed to a separation that was like
a knife in her heart" (XXIV, 311) from her beloved Amerigo,
but also to perpetual ignorance—for she will never know how
much Maggie knows. One of Maggie's most insidious stratagems
is to rely upon Charlotte's ignorance to restrain her, to keep her
defenseless. And yet the reader is not to accuse Maggie of malice
or cruelty; she takes the only effective course. As Maggie has
suggested, there must be those to suffer and pay for the evil of
all. For, though in The Golden Bowl James dramatizes the sup-
pression of evil by good, he does not alter a truth of his earlier
fiction—that evil is ultimately irremediable and permanent, in its
effects if not in its intensity.

    F. W. Dupee states that "The Golden Bowl is an unsparing
picture of the inevitable strain of private life . . . ." [29] The private

life becomes a strain to all the members of the Verver circle because each, especially Maggie, seeks desperately to reconcile private differences with the social unit. James's repeated implication is that society necessarily entails some violation of individual rights. In reality society is composed of aggressor and prey. In appearance, however, it consists in the forms of intercourse which suggest equability and happiness. Though false, appearance has a certain reality of its own: to James's mind organized society, based on culture and manners, provides a common ground for communication and association, and a valuable means of experience. In *The Golden Bowl* Maggie seeks to preserve the appearance of society, and James is sympathetic with her goal.

James's emphasis is on the sinister rather than the beautiful aspects of society, on its reality rather than its appearance. He dramatizes a condition in which human relations are made impossible. The morally isolated members are held together by the weakest of bonds. Each feels the horror of the unspoken reality, which each perceives—though some more clearly than others—and each is compelled to preserve the appearance of tranquility, to remain silent. Superficially, Maggie, the Prince, Charlotte, and Mr. Verver give the appearance of harmony and bliss:

> The merely specious description of their case would have been that, after being for a long time, as a family, delightfully, uninterruptedly happy, they had still a new felicity to discover; a felicity for which, blessedly, her father's appetite and her own in particular had been kept fresh and grateful (XXIV, 72–73).

The actual is most horrible, and its evil most felt, because of its discrepancy with the apparent. In the late chapters Maggie sees only "terrors and shames and ruins" instead of what might appear "serenities and dignities and decencies" (XXIV, 236). Her vision of evil is far more intense than her first awareness of her husband's infidelity, for she is confronted with "the horror of finding evil seated all at its ease where she had only dreamed of good; the horror of the thing hideously *behind*, behind so much trusted, so much pretended, nobleness, cleverness, tenderness" (XXIV, 237).

Unlike most of her predecessors, Maggie is not permanently

severed from life by her encounter with evil. Rather she comes to accept it as an unavoidable element of experience and also to revise her childish delusion that one should seek only personal happiness, which she had considered not only eminently good, but also eminently obtainable. The rapidly maturing Maggie finds that "any deep-seated passion has its pangs as well as its joys, and that we are made by its aches and its anxieties most richly conscious of it" (XXIV, 7).

Like Milly Theale, Maggie acquires and exercises spiritual love, which replaces her limited and dangerous love for her father. Maggie can "bear anything," she tells Fanny Assingham, not for the love of her father or of her husband, but "For love" (XXIV, 115–116). Maggie's love shelters her from the selfish emotions of jealously and resentment, but it makes it impossible for her to escape the anguish of a knowledge of evil. As her love is general and universal, so must her sense of evil be deep and inclusive. If Maggie's heroic deeds for love counterbalance the force of evil, they never diminish it. Significantly, the Prince, who is associated with an ultimate in human evil by his Italian ancestry, and not Maggie, has the most appropriate word. He tells his wife, "Everything's terrible, cara—in the heart of man" (XXIV, 349).

CHAPTER FIVE

The Last Tales: The Appalled Appalling

THE dominant concern in James's fiction is knowledge. James repeatedly explored means by which the individual might develop his moral and aesthetic consciousness. In the beginning the school of experience is Europe, the spiritual testing ground where Newman and Isabel Archer attain a high degree of moral sensibility. In the nineties the setting is London, hideous in its selfish materialism, a world which has renounced the aesthetic and traditional past for the modern values of money, efficiency, and lust. In this shallow society the James protagonist—now a child—encounters only pain, with none of the benefits of civilization. His acquired knowledge—Maisie's for example—is mainly of the moral inadequacy of society. In *The Ambassadors*, *The Wings of the Dove*, and *The Golden Bowl*, European civilization is not vulgar, but sterile. The impotent grace of Mme. de Vionnet and Prince Amerigo and the shrill beauty of Palazzo Leporelli and Matcham are James's symbols of a past without meaning in the present. In these novels the personal drama reflects social disintegration, the ultimate betrayal of the past. The veil of pretense, lending beauty to corruption, is ripped aside with the climax of each novel: Mme. de Vionnet and Chad in the boat, the cataclysmic storm in Venice, the sinister bridge game at Fawns.

James's symbols of social collapse retain their validity in the works that follow, for these stories show James's concern with the possibilities of spiritual expansion outside a social context. The only milieu given in these works is the degenerate money culture of America; in most of the tales there is no society at all, simply the abstracted individual. Especially in "A Round of Visits" and "The Bench of Desolation," but to a degree in the other tales too, James dramatizes the plight of the man of sensibilities in a naked world, institutionally and culturally bankrupt. The bleak expanse of water and sky before which Herbert Dodd spends most of his life might well represent the ruined, blasted world that provides the setting for the last fiction in general. The characters exist in tight and restricted places: small hotel rooms, dingy seaside resorts, sealed-off eighteenth-century houses, empty New York homes. Each is at the beginning homeless and dislocated; the dominant movement is wandering and search through vacant rooms and aimless streets.

What these stories show is that nothing—not society or civilization certainly—can define the self except the self. To this purpose James's regular themes are reconsidered. The unspoken plea continues to be "Live, live all you can," but fulfillment now comes directly through self-understanding. Thus the lifelong theme of "what might have been," which reaches its culmination in Strether, is now the theme of what always has been. The terror in the ghost visions of Spencer Brydon and Ralph Pendrel derives from their perception not of what they might have become, but of what they are.

James's final stories assimilate two of his preoccupying themes of the nineties: that is, the destructiveness of egotism, which is treated most pointedly in "The Beast in the Jungle," and the revelation of unsuspected depravity in the personality, the main theme of the ghost stories of the middle period. The two themes are brought together in the character of the detached observer, a characteristic James type, but one which he treated in mid-career with much less sympathy than in earlier years. In the course of their stories, John Marcher, George Stransom, and the narrators of "The Aspern Papers" and The Sacred Fount are brought face to face with their egotism; each emerges as a man possessed by an evil much like Hawthorne's "Unforgivable Sin." Stransom is saved by his recognition, but the rest become increasingly more separate from others, as they withdraw into their own worlds.

The theme of the recognition of personal evil is obliquely suggested in the often-quoted nightmare passage in A Small Boy and Others. According to the dream, set in the Galerie d' Apollon of the Louvre, James puts to flight a monster who had a moment fore horrified and pursued him. James concludes that "I, in my appalled state, was probably still more appalling than the awful agent, creature or presence . . . ." [1] The resemblance of the action of the nightmare to the action of "The Jolly Corner" has often been pointed out. But the pattern of the appalled man turning out to be more appalling than the monster who confronts him is a fairly common structural principle in James's fiction after 1897. The governess in "The Turn of the Screw," for instance, is a case of the appalled person—she is driven to panic by what the demons are doing to the children—becoming herself the appalling one—she terrifies both children and to some degree causes the death of one. The pattern of the nightmare is duplicated more precisely in *The Ambassadors*; it is as if the governess terrifies the ghosts; here Strether expects to be dismayed by Chad and outraged by his mistress, but he instead frightens them into withdrawal. His New England conscience is a greater force for evil than European impropriety.

It is through his use—possibly unconscious—of the motif of the appalled appalling that James converts a moral principle into aesthetic form. The dramatic revelation of character exposes the inner evil of the one who has had the reader's sympathy. The pattern operates in James's last works with a simplicity that somewhat conceals their resemblance to earlier works. James has eliminated all but the essence of the theme—the sudden revelation of personal pride. Not only is the elaborate social context gone, but the supporting cast, the human antagonists, are reduced in importance. It is as if *The Awkward Age* were written with the emphasis on Vanderbank only and Mrs. Brook not at all. In these bare and intense tales the theme of experience has undergone a strange mutation. To experience life one must come to a full knowledge of the self, without the enriching agency of a social framework. In each case the central character must return to the roots of his being.

In "A Round of Visits" (1910) the standard reversal from appalled to appalling is associated with the theme of suffering, so that we are left in the end with the impression of a bleak and noisy world in which meaning resides in suffering only, that of the victim and the victimizer, who share a moral bond that the others, the barbarous and the vapid, cannot experience. Typical of James's last protagonists, Mark Monteith is a long-time American expatriate who returns to find the New York community of his youth a pile of "broken bits." [2] The stable and responsible society he remembers has degenerated to a gaudy anarchy of selfish women. When he returns to New York he learns that his best friend, Phil Bloodgood, has betrayed his trust and absconded with the money Monteith has asked him to invest. Monteith is so appalled by the treachery that he feels he must have someone share his pain. However, everyone he encounters has a tale of woe of his own, though these complaints are petty and banal. Monteith is finally driven to search out an old companion, Newton Winch, whom he had never liked and always considered dull and boorish. It emerges that Winch, like the characters in *The Sacred Fount*, has undergone a physical, emotional, and intellectual transformation, so that he is now a man of sensibility and intelligence. While Monteith unburdens himself to Winch, who provides him the sympathy he seeks, it becomes apparent that Winch has done to someone else what Bloodgood has done to Monteith. In Winch, Monteith sees Bloodgood. His vision changes from that of Bloodgood causing him pain to that of himself pursuing and paining Bloodgood. The imagery of the hunt, which dominates the nightmare passage, is used with similar effect in "A Round of Visits": "our hero found himself on his feet again, under the influence of a sudden failure of everything but horror. . . . It was as if a far-borne sound of the hue and cry, a vision of his old friend hunted and at bay, had suddenly broken in . . . ." [3] In an act of compassion Monteith escapes his own agony to accept Winch's, and by extension Bloodgood's. In doing so, Monteith, like his predecessors George Stransom, Milly Theale, and Maggie Verver, purges himself of the pride of separateness, which usually assumes the guise of betrayed innocence in James, to unite in sympathy with his betrayer. Winch, on the other hand, and presumably Bloodgood too, unites with the one he has betrayed. His transformed personality suggests the effect of disinterested suffering: it has widened the moral vision and purified the sensibility. Winch's burden of suffering proves unbearable, however, and he kills himself.[4] At the end of the story Monteith is left with the pain alone.

The story suggests that the ultimate experience is suffering itself—that love is a community of suffering, that guilt and innocence are negligible distinctions within the larger territory of pain, for the pain originates in the being and action of all.

"The Bench of Desolation" (1910) has a like theme, although this story is acted out not against the background of a hollow society but in a social vacuum. The characters are completely isolated; there are not even artificial relationships which can be said to constitute a society. The two main figures in "The Bench of Desolation" are homeless, desolate people. In the beginning each sees nothing but his own suffering, and in the end nothing but the other's suffering. Here again is the purposeful ambiguity of guilt and innocence, with the apparently victimized Herbert Dodd made to re-see himself and accept his own guilt.

Dodd breaks his engagement to Kate Cookham, and when Kate demands reparation, Dodd feels all the more confident that he has acted wisely. Kate, to him, has an "appalling nature";[5] when Kate tells him that she will take his breach of promise to the courts Dodd goes into bankruptcy to meet her price and avoid facing the vulgar publicity and possible scandal of a legal battle. He marries Nan Drury, whom he finds a woman of taste, quite the opposite of Kate Cookham. However, he is so broken by the demands of Kate for reparation that his wife and children die. It is here that he is haunted by the fear that Kate had no case against him, that there was no obligation on his part to pay her, that he sacrificed his family to his pride, to what he always considered his "natural taste."[6] When, much later, Kate returns, she appears, like Newton Winch, totally transformed, "another and a totally different person," "a 'real' lady."[7] Kate offers Dodd a large sum of money, the fruits of years of penurious living, hard work at a series of distasteful jobs, and careful investment of Dodd's payment. She too has suffered, in an effort to redeem the past; in abject humility she presents Dodd the testament of her pain and love. Dodd's pride for a time restrains him from acceptance of the gift, but eventually he realizes his role in their mutual woe. As the story ends, "She was beside him on the bench of desolation."[8]

It is apparent that several themes of "A Round of Visits" are present in "The Bench of Desolation." Herbert Dodd, like Mark Monteith, must endure the desolation, first, of a sense of separateness, the isolation brought on by pride and righteousness, and, second, the desolation of common agony. Like Monteith, Dodd is the pursued man who must eventually perceive the evil within himself. The great sin is not what Kate Cookham has done to Dodd, but what Dodd, through pride, has done to Nan Drury. In the same way, it is Monteith's pain that makes living unendurable for Winch and brings him to suicide. In each case, however, with self-knowledge, an acceptance of one's role in the common human sorrow,[9] there comes, not relief, but a deepening of consciousness.[10]

The structural opposition of appearance and reality reveals the ambiguity of guilt and innocence in the tale. Dodd has habitually evaluated himself and the two women in his life as persons of fixed moral natures: in his righteousness he esteems his own superiority to the common herd and Nan Drury's "God-given distinction of type," and scorns Kate's "native indelicacy," "her essential excess of will and destitution of scruple." [11] In accepting Kate's love, Dodd must stoop to vulgarity, renounce his egotistic aloofness from the degrading, and without qualification accept the sins of his past. Kate too must rise above the humiliation of being a rejected fiancée to do all for love. What Dodd takes to be her natural coarseness is refined through years of self-abasing atonement. Likewise, "beautiful, gentle-tender-souled Nan" [12] soon degenerates into a dull, spiteful woman under the pressures of poverty. The meaning of these three reversals from what Dodd believes qualities according to nature is not just that Dodd's pride has distorted his vision, but also that the real self can only emerge through the suffering of desolation. Such pain either refines or destroys.

In "The Jolly Corner" (1908) the dream incident is literally used, and in virtually all its details, especially in Spencer Brydon's routing of the monster who has terrified him. The standard explanation, that Brydon exorcises the ghost he might have become by acknowledging it, does not account for the fright of the

beast, who is as thoroughly vanquished by the real Brydon as is
the monster in the nightmare by James.[13] The fact that Brydon
has for thirty years derived his income from his New York
houses, "living in luxury on *those* ill-gotten gains" (XVII, 444),
as Alice Staverton puts it, and that Brydon, like John Marcher
and Herbert Dodd, has sheltered himself from the love of a
woman—in this case, Alice Staverton—suggest that there is a
positive as well as a negative beast within him. The actual Brydon
is more appalling than the self he has avoided becoming. Brydon's
pride in escaping from his past parallels Monteith's feeling of
outrage and Dodd's comfort in his taste; like the others Brydon
must re-examine his past: he must see the deadening vanity of his
"selfish frivolous scandalous life" (XVII, 450).

In *The Sense of the Past* (1917) James follows the pattern of
the nightmare almost as closely as in "The Jolly Corner"; however, in the novel he seems little concerned with the moral implications so prominent in the short story. By comparison, *The
Sense of the Past* is an elaborate mechanical exercise, a tour de
force in which the fantastic psychological complexity of Ralph
Pendrel's assuming the identity of a man living a hundred years
ago and at the same time retaining his own identity is explored
for its own sake. The dramatic emphasis is on Pendrel's alteration
from a man frightened by a world he cannot comprehend to a
source of fright himself, but James's extensive notes indicate his
major concern to have been merely the rarefied problems of
Pendrel's incredible situation. One can only speculate what James
might have made of the novel had he lived to complete it.

The opening chapter presents a situation like those in other
works of the last phase: a man renounces life in the present,
specifically marriage, to engage in an exclusively private pursuit.
In this way Pendrel's rejection of Aurora Coyne for his sense of
the past recalls Dodd's rejection of Kate Cookham for pride in
taste and Spencer Brydon's rejection of Alice Staverton for cultivated idleness in Europe. The given situation is contrived and
mechanical: Aurora Coyne will not marry Pendrel unless he remains in America. Yet the effect is to pose Pendrel with the conflict of love and selfhood.

This theme is not fully developed in either the novel or the notes, but certain suggestions of what James had in mind are present. Several issues emerge: first, Pendrel creates in the inhabitants of the 1820 world a malaise, a terror which is the effect not of what Pendrel does, but of what he is—a man of the twentieth century; second, Pendrel's great fear is that he may be permanently lost in the past. The point may be that Pendrel is seeing the horror of his real self, which is evil simply in its detachment from any personal relationship, and that through his experience Pendrel finds that real identity can be acquired only through acceptance of the present. "It wasn't for Ralph as if he had lost himself," James writes, ". . . but much rather as if in respect to what he most cared for he had never found himself till now" (XXVI, 66). Ralph can discover the present only after discovering the past. He can live fully through others only —through marriage to Aurora Coyne specifically—and not at all through his retreat into the ego through the past.

Pendrel's pride is reflected not only in his inevitable differences from the older society, but also in his aloofness from the world in which he finds himself. Perception is his sole mode of being; he disregards the responsibilities attendant upon his position—albeit a false one—as relative and prospective husband. According to the notes, Pendrel betrays his alter ego: he "has done the other fellow a violence, has wronged the personality of the other fellow *in him*, in himself, Ralph, by depriving him of the indicated, the consonant union with the fine handsome desirable girl whom the 1820 man would perfectly and successfully have been in love with . . ." (XXVI, 322). James projected that Nan Midmore, who loves Ralph's alter ego without being loved by him, and who attracts Ralph far more than his alter ego's fiancée, shall in some undefined manner "liberate" Ralph from the past: "she gives him up for what is to herself utterly nothing, nothing but the exaltation of sacrifice" (XXVI, 349). Nan's sacrifice, in some ways like Kate Cookham's, would seem to point up by contrast the egotism of Ralph's purely intellectual involvement in other lives.

Thus we may speculate that if *The Sense of the Past* were to have a meaning beyond its fantastic plot, it might have been a reworking of the theme of isolation and self-discovery. In the past

Ralph realizes he is cut off from life; he is made to wish to return to the present, to subdue the self in the experience of love.

The remaining works of James's last phase differ somewhat from the prevailing pattern in that they are fundamentally comic. Especially in "The Velvet Glove" and "Mora Montravers" and less obviously in "Crapy Cornelia" and *The Ivory Tower*, human differences suggest comic incongruity rather than occasions for pain. Significantly, however, these primarily satiric works derive their structures from the same concerns which inform the other late tales.

In theme, the slightest of the stories, "The Velvet Glove" (1909), resembles "The Real Thing"; James, however, has added the pride of the artist, whose vanity permits him to be fooled by an impressive-looking but vacuous woman. "Mora Montravers" (1909) is more typical of James's late work. The story is seen through the eyes of an aesthetic idler, Traffle, an egotist interested in others solely as sources of comic diversion. His wife, Jane, a rigid moralist, is appalled when their niece, Mora, leaves them to live with a bohemian artist, Puddick. What occurs is that each character except Traffle is shown to be considerably more moral and intelligent than he first appeared: Mora and Puddick are quite innocent; the puritanical Jane retreats from her morality of respectability to befriend the artist. The egotist, however, is left unchanged. Having at first esteemed himself the sole person with perception and integrity, he finds himself in the end the only person with neither.

For the purposes of comedy, James has cut short the motif of the appalled appalling. He has been more concerned with the humorous possibilities of hidden character and self-discovery. In "The Velvet Glove" and "Mora Montravers," everyone turns out to be quite different from what he first seemed. But these stories conclude with social reconciliation. Furthermore, the man of pride is observer only; he is engaged in no personal crisis; his vanity has no opportunity to affect others.

"Crapy Cornelia" and *The Ivory Tower* repeat the central situation of "The Jolly Corner" and "A Round of Visits." The American expatriate, after years of unproductive leisure in Europe, returns to America, where he is oppressed by the vulgar materialism of modern American civilization. White-Mason in "Crapy Cornelia" (1909) plans to propose to the dazzling and eminently modern Mrs. Worthingham, but decides against it after he meets a friend from his youth, Cornelia Rasch, whose poverty and age do not disguise her refinement. Through the contrast White-Mason sees the indelicacy of Mrs. Worthingham. There is pride in his condescension toward Cornelia's absurd appearance, but it is overcome through his final preference of her to the younger, richer, and prettier Mrs. Worthingham. White-Mason, like Brydon, is a homeless man who finally abandons the idleness of life in Europe and the barbarism of life in America to accept the comfort of a human relation. In "Crapy Cornelia," however, there is no suggestion of the unconscious sin of dissociation from social responsibility; there is merely the comic manipulation of the appearance and reality theme in the contrast between Cornelia and Mrs. Worthingham.

The Ivory Tower (1917) repeats the theme of "A Round of Visits," though with much less intensity. Graham Fielder, who has inherited a large amount of money, asks Horton Vint to watch over it for him. Vint, like Phil Bloodgood, betrays his trust and steals much of the money. Fielder is not appalled though, for he recognizes immediately his own complicity in the crime— through presenting the temptation, through his scornful unconcern with the mechanics of investment and banking, and most of all through his association with money immorally acquired. Like Monteith, but with nothing like his suffering, Fielder is brought to compassion for his betrayer. Fielder finally abandons the money entirely, presumably leaving much of it to Vint; but James's notes do not suggest he is to share the kind of moral bond with his betrayer that unites Monteith and Bloodgood.

It appears that James can conceive of no satisfactory social relationship for his last protagonists. The most tenuous association with the plunder of the American robber barons, with "the awful game of grab" (XXV, 33), involves Spencer Brydon, Mark Monteith, and Graham Fielder in immorality. Furthermore, American society is so vulgar and insipid that social intercourse is necessarily unrewarding. On the other hand, James implies that the American can find little that is permanently valuable in Europe. Europe is a negation: it lacks the oppressiveness of America; life for the American in Europe is "wasted." Ralph Pendrel's inability to live in the past typifies the general impossibility of the American's benefitting from the traditional. Nor do the protagonists find in the persons they love the values of a civilization: Newton Winch and Aurora Coyne cannot be defined as products of a class or a culture; Claire de Cintré and Prince Amerigo cannot be defined otherwise. To the late James there is no salvation beyond the private life. Human love, whether it be the compassion in desolation of Kate Cookham and Herbert Dodd or the more conventional attachment of Graham Fielder and Rosanna Gaw, is the sole means of existence in the empty world of James's last tales.

Conclusion

According to its traditional meaning, the concept "evil" implies the existence of absolute moral standards. In modern times, however, "evil" is most often but a convenient term loosely applied to any form or agent of injury and pain; rarely is it intended to suggest a deviation from a transcendent and unchanging moral order. Since the early eighteenth century, the notion of uniform standards of "good" on the levels of personal, social, and political behavior has lost much ground to more relativistic views of morality.

In this respect, Henry James's relation to his age is curious. James, I think, assumes absolute standards of good and evil; his approach to morality is reactionary—closer to that of Shakespeare and Milton than that of Zola and Dreiser. Yet, if the moral code is an absolute one in James's fiction, his characters perceive it only in the most subjective way. They apprehend both good and evil through the "moral sense," ultimately a faculty of spiritual intuition. The reason is not just that in the stage of history treated by James there is no uniformity of moral standards or any religious, political, or social body which gives voice and authority to common notions of right and wrong, but that James in part shares the modern skepticism. There can be no externally derived moral knowledge. Evil exists absolutely, but hardly objectively.

Because evil is an absolute to James, it must be distinguished from mere failures in manners or violations of conventions, though it exists in close relation to extremely formal, and relative, social standards. James presumes a traditional conception of evil, yet dramatizes it in rarefied social conflicts. In this respect he can be said to urbanize Hawthorne. It is a tribute to James's range and

168

his sophistication that he retains the absolute moral specifications of religious orthodoxy in his worldly settings, his psychologically complex characters, and his various uses of literary realism.

In attempting to elaborate this view, I have used the term "evil" to refer to a multitude of characters and situations. I am well aware that the term itself may be misleading; it has unavoidable connotations of the grave and the sinister, and can be qualified only with some awkwardness. Though evil in James is an absolute in that it transcends convention, not every individual, situation, or action which partakes of that evil should be considered absolutely malignant. Though I have considered Daisy Miller's ignorance a moral failing, and therefore a condition of evil, I have no wish to group her with the Gilbert Osmonds and Peter Quints. The Gothic, melodramatic, and fundamentalist associations of the word "evil" make it an especially cumbersome approach to the subtleties of James. Evil is real and significant in his fiction, but it is rarely sinister and never grim. Not only is his world one of beauty, honor, and humor, but evil itself is frequently identified with these qualities.

The fact that James takes evil both seriously and absolutely is probably one of the main reasons for the great interest mid-twentieth-century critics and readers have taken in his works. It is not accidental that the increase in James's appeal has coincided with the rising popularity of Melville, Hawthorne, and Emily Dickinson. A greater religious seriousness—to some, a "neo-orthodoxy"—and a disillusionment with political and scientific solutions to human anxiety are at least as influential in the James revival as modern criticism's high regard for fictional technique. In the twenties and thirties no respected critic took the word "sin" at its traditional valuation; but the day of Mencken and Parrington has clearly ended.

Of course, in spite of its orthodox elements, James's view of evil is not rigidly or exclusively Christian. James's conception of the reality and irremediability of sin is common to Christianity, especially the Puritan version. But there is no hint of dogma in James's fiction, no theology, and no divine grace. James's works can never be considered Christian in the way that Greene's or Mauriac's are. In addition, the view of evil which James derived from the Christian tradition is supplemented, though not softened, by elements derived from the American traditions of ethical pragmatism and transcendentalism (its psychology, not its ontology).

If modern criticism has discovered James's link to the New England past, through Hawthorne, it has also discovered his link to the twentieth century, through T. S. Eliot. Stephen Spender in particular has illuminated James's closeness to Eliot, Yeats, Auden, and the other poets and novelists distressed by the religious disorientation of modern man. Particularly appropriate to the present study is Spender's view that in James's late novels, "Once the situation is provided the actors cannot behave otherwise. Their only compensation is that by the use of their intelligence, by their ability to understand, to love, and to suffer, they may to some extent atone for the evil which is simply the evil of the modern world. It is these considerations that make his later books parables of modern Western civilization." [1]

These remarks are suggestive, though not, I think, completely accurate. In James, the breakdown of western civilization—the split between the forms of the past and modern selfhood, primarily greed—leads to a condition in which the moral intelligence finds itself totally isolated. The loss of belief in James's fiction is not a denial of religion, but of traditional secular civilization. Beyond this, however, it is questionable that the evil in James's last novels is "simply the evil of the modern world." It is both more and less than this. These novels are richly symbolic, but hardly parables. Their historical meaning develops from their psychological realism. James's vision of things is almost always dual, perceptive of the private moral aspects of any given situation, and also of the relevance of "the special case" to the larger context of the western world. Though in a tale like "The Beast in the Jungle" there is little or no suggestion of national or international themes, most of James's works to some obvious degree extend beyond the private problem to the larger social condition. Evil is above all personal; if it is an attribute of a civilization or symptomatic of social disintegration, it remains the concern of the private man.

Finally, of course, James is an artist. We do not turn to his

fiction for solutions to the problem of evil or of any problem. As
Philip Rahv has wisely said, "it is hardly the writer's business to
stand in for the scientist and the philosopher." [2] James especially
seeks to reflect the fullness and complexity of experience through
the ordering agency of art. Though it is a commonplace in James
criticism, the most fitting conclusion to this study is surely an
insistence on James's conviction that the experience represented
in a novel can only be that which is bristling, felt, dramatized.
"The high price of the novel as a literary form" is

> its power not only, while preserving that form with close-
> ness, to range through all the differences of the individual
> relation to its general subject-matter, all the varieties of
> outlook on life, of disposition to reflect and project, created
> by conditions that are never the same from man to man (or,
> as far as that goes, from woman to woman), but positively
> to appear more true to its character in proportion as it strains,
> or tends to burst, with a latent extravagance, its mould.[3]

Ultimately the element of evil remains an indistinct and undefined
component of all that comprises "life" in the work of art.

NOTES

Works referred to in the Preface, listed in order of reference:

Paul, Siwek, *The Philosophy of Evil* (New York: Ronald Press, 1951). Henry, James, *The Complete Plays of Henry James*, ed. by Leon Edel (London: Rupert Hart-Davis, 1949).

CHAPTER ONE

The Consciousness of Evil

[1] Charles Baudelaire, *French Poets and Novelists* (London: Macmillan & Co., 1919), p. 61.

[2] "The Aesthetic Idealism of Henry James," *The Question of Henry James*, ed. F. W. Dupee (New York: Henry Holt & Co.), p. 87.

[3] "Maule's Well; or Henry James and the Relation of Morals to Manners," *Maule's Curse* (Norfolk, Conn.: New Directions, 1938), pp. 187–216.

[4] Graham Greene, *The Lost Childhood and Other Essays* (London: Heineman, 1951), p. 26.

[5] *Letters to A. C. Benson and Auguste Monod*, ed. E. F. Benson (London: Elkin Mathews & Marrot, 1930), p. 35. In another letter, however, James seems to minimize the power of evil. When he wrote Vernon Lee about her first novel (dedicated to James), he criticized her "want of perspective and proportion. You are really too savage with your painters and poets and dilettanti; *life* is less criminal, less obnoxious, less objectionable, less crude, more *bon enfant*, more mixed and casual, and even in its most offensive manifestations, more *pardonable*, than the unholy circle with which you have surrounded your heroine" (*The Selected Letters of Henry James*, edited with an introduction by Leon Edel [London: Rupert Hart-Davis, 1956], p. 238). Here James is abhorring Gothic excesses, which overemphasize and exaggerate the noxiousness of evil. James cautions against the artist's falsifying reality and thereby offending "our general sense of 'the way things happen'" (*The Art of the Novel: Critical Prefaces by Henry James*, with an introduction by Richard P. Blackmur [New York: Charles Scribner's Sons, 1934], p. 34). James seems critical of Vernon Lee's use of fiction as a vehicle for moral instruction rather than as a reflection of life: "You have proposed to yourself too little to make a firm, compact work—and you have been too much in a moral passion. . . . Morality is hot—but art is icy" (*Selected Letters*, p. 207).

Notes 173

6 "Henry James," *Literary History of the United States,* ed. R. E. Spiller and others (New York: Macmillan Co., 1948), II, 1060.

7 All volume and page references cited in the text are to *The Novels and Tales of Henry James,* New York Edition (New York: Charles Scribner's Sons, 1907–17). I have used the text of the New York Edition for the discussions of all the works included therein; however, this study is not confined to the works included in this edition.

8 "Emerson," *The Art of Fiction and Other Essays,* introduction by Morris Roberts (New York: Oxford University Press, 1948), p. 224.

9 *Hawthorne* (New York: Harper & Bros., 1880), p. 99.

10 *The Letters of Henry James,* selected and edited by Percy Lubbock (New York: Charles Scribner's Sons, 1920), I, 100.

11 *Notes of a Son and Brother* (New York: Charles Scribner's Sons, 1914), p. 224.

12 "Ivan Turgenieff," *French Poets and Novelists,* p. 250.

13 *Apologia pro Vita Sua* (New York: Sheed and Ward, 1947), p. 220.

14 *Faith and History* (New York: Charles Scribner's Sons, 1951), p. 120.

15 Katherine Hoskins, "Henry James and the Future of the Novel," *Sewanee Review,* LIV (January–March, 1946), 98, calls attention to James's habit of neglecting the ordinary emotional reaction to death. Of *The Wings of the Dove,* she writes, "seldom in literature has a death taken place with [such] pagan avoidance of the normal thoughts that attend death."

16 Janet Adam Smith, ed., *Henry James and Robert Louis Stevenson: A Record of Friendship and Criticism* (London: Rupert Hart-Davis, 1948), p. 33 (introduction).

17 "The Sacred Fount," *Kenyon Review,* IV (Autumn, 1942), 333.

18 *A Small Boy and Others* (New York: Charles Scribner's Sons, 1913), pp. 347–348.

19 *Hawthorne,* p. 4.

20 *The Art of the Novel,* pp. 64–65.

21 James's American protagonists live "happily and freely, by spiritual, ethical, and intellectual values"; they have a "firm belief in the goodness of human nature," and they aspire "toward the higher life, the purest humanities, the most spontaneous expression" (Katherine Anne Porter, "The Days Before," *Kenyon Review,* V [Autumn, 1943], 488).

In *The Comic Sense of Henry James* (London: Chatto & Windus, 1960), Richard Poirier calls Isabel Archer "an Emersonian Becky Sharp" (p. 217) and fully examines the significance of Emersonianism in *The Portrait of a Lady.*

22 "The Choice So Freely Made," *The New Republic* (Sept. 26, 1955), p. 27.

23 James's observations about Zola are relevant: "Zola had had inordinately to simplify—had had to leave out the life of the soul, practically, and confine himself to the life of the instincts, of the more immediate passions, such as can be easily and promptly caught in the fact. He had had, in a word, to confine himself almost entirely to the impulses and agitations that men and women are possessed by in common, and to take them as exhibited in mass and number, so that, being writ larger, they might likewise be more easily read" (*The Question of Our Speech and The Lesson of Balzac* [Boston and New York: Houghton Mifflin Co., 1905], pp. 91–92).

[24] See for example Elizabeth Stevenson, *The Crooked Corridor: A Study of Henry James* (New York: Macmillan Co., 1949), p. 89; and Philip Rahv, "The Heiress of All the Ages," *Image and Idea* (New York: New Directions, 1949), p. 56n.

[25] Nathaniel Hawthorne, *The Scarlet Letter*, in *The Complete Novels and Selected Tales of Nathaniel Hawthorne*, ed. Norman Holmes Pearson (New York: Modern Library, 1937), p. 200.

[26] Osborn Andreas, *Henry James and the Expanding Horizon* (Seattle: University of Washington Press, 1948), p. 22.

[27] *Hawthorne*, p. 132.

[28] In saying that the Jamesian villain is realistic, I do not wish to suggest that his sinfulness can be explained by naturalistic causes; only rarely and partially does evil originate in physical or mental conditions. Lyon N. Richardson, *Henry James: Representative Selections, with Introduction, Bibliography and Notes* (New York: American Book Co., 1941), falls into the error of explaining evil in James as a result of physiological and psychical disorders: "It is a general rule in James's works that when evil appears there is manifest also the sense of a disordered mind which tacitly explains but does not condone the sin" (p. xxiii).

[29] "Marius Bewley, Hawthorne and Henry James," *The Complex Fate* (London: Chatto and Windus, 1952), pp. 11–31, describes in some detail the similarities and differences between *The Blithedale Romance* and *The Bostonians*, pointing out how James converts Hawthorne's Gothic elements into credible characters and situations.

[30] *Notes of a Son and Brother*, p. 7.

[31] *The American Adam* (Chicago: University of Chicago Press, 1955), p. 153.

[32] See Robert Bechtold Heilman, "*The Turn of the Screw* as Poem," *Forms of Modern Fiction*, ed. William Van O'Connor (Minneapolis: University of Minnesota Press, 1948), pp. 211–228.

[33] See Jacques Barzun, "Henry James, Melodramatist," *The Question of Henry James*, pp. 254–266; and Leo B. Levy, *Versions of Melodrama: A Study of the Fiction and Drama of Henry James, 1865–1897* (Berkeley and Los Angeles: University of California Press, 1957).

[34] "Henry James," *Readers and Writers* (New York: A. A. Knopf, 1922), p. 12.

[35] *The Art of the Novel*, pp. 175–176.

[36] "Henry James and the Trapped Spectator," *Explorations* (New York: G. W. Stewart, 1947), p. 179.

CHAPTER TWO

Evil and the International Theme

[1] *The Art of the Novel*, p. 198.

[2] *A Small Boy and Others*, pp. 122, 161, 234.

[3] *The American Adam*, pp. 152–155.

[4] *Hawthorne*, p. 3.

[5] *Notes of a Son and Brother*, p. 458.

[6] *The Novels and Stories of Henry James*, ed. Percy Lubbock (London: Macmillan & Co., 1921), III, 74.

⁷ *Novels and Stories,* III, 35, 38, 39.

⁸ *Novels and Stories,* III, 77–78.

⁹ As is suggested in Chapter I, James is a moral pragmatist. For discussion, see Eliseo Vivas, "Henry and William (Two Notes)," *Kenyon Review,* V (Autumn, 1943), 580–594; and Joseph Firebaugh, "The Pragmatism of Henry James," *Virginia Quarterly Review,* XXVII (Summer, 1951), 419–435. For a discussion of James's attitude toward the lie, see Marius Bewley, "Appearance and Reality in Henry James," *The Complex Fate,* pp. 79–113.

¹⁰ *Henry James* (New York: Henry Holt & Co., 1916), p. 42.

¹¹ *The Bostonians* (New York: Dial Press, 1945), pp. 12–13, 25, 149.

¹² "On Henry James," *The Question of Henry James,* p. 113.

¹³ "Henry James, the Satirist," *Hound and Horn,* VII (April–May, 1934), 516.

¹⁴ *The History of the English Novel* (London: H. F. and G. Witherby, 1938), IX, 516.

¹⁵ "Lady Windermere's Fan," *Salome, The Importance of Being Earnest, Lady Windermere's Fan* (New York: Boni and Liveright, 1919), p. 141.

¹⁶ "Nature," *Selected Prose and Poetry* (New York: Rinehart & Co., 1950), p. 12.

¹⁷ *The Art of the Novel,* p. 274.

¹⁸ "The Enchanted Kingdom of Henry James," *The Wind Blew from the West* (New York: Harper & Bros.), p. 93.

¹⁹ *A Small Boy and Others,* pp. 50–51.

²⁰ *Craft and Character in Modern Fiction* (New York: Viking Press), p. 123.

²¹ *A Small Boy and Others,* pp. 14, 47.

²² *The Pilgrimage of Henry James* (New York: E. P. Dutton & Co., 1925), p. 29.

²³ It has been pointed out often that James regards orphanage, like wealth, an essential condition of freedom for his feminine protagonists. Isabel Archer, Fleda Vetch, and Milly Theale are parentless; the parent in James is invariably a severe limitation, as, for example, with Catherine Sloper, Nanda Brookenham, and Maggie Verver. Marius Bewley, "Henry James and 'Life,'" *The Eccentric Design* (New York: Columbia University Press, 1959), in discussing the short story "Europe," observes that "The Image of the Mother, usually a life-symbol, is used in this story as a symbol of life-in-death . . ." (p. 237). Nonetheless, orphanage has a double meaning in James: in my consideration of *The Wings of the Dove,* I try to show that James identifies the catastrophes that have devastated Milly Theale's family with the doom that awaits Milly. The same basic situation exists, though less obviously, in many of James's works.

²⁴ *Henry James: Man and Author* (Boston and New York: Houghton Mifflin Co., 1927), pp. 249–250.

²⁵ *Notes of a Son and Brother,* p. 491.

²⁶ *Washington Square* (New York: Harper & Bros., 1894), p. 244.

²⁷ See *The Art of the Novel,* p. 187: "if I hadn't had, on behalf of the American character, the negative aspects to deal with, I should practically, and given the limits of my range, have had no aspects at all."

²⁸ *The Crooked Corridor,* p. 33.

²⁹ "The Enchanted Kingdom of Henry James," p. 107.

³⁰ This point has been stressed by Richard Chase in his study of *The Por-*

176

THE IMAGINATION OF DISASTER

trait of a Lady; see *The American Novel and Its Tradition* (New York: Doubleday Anchor Books, 1957), pp. 117–138.

[31] *The Great Tradition* (New York: George W. Stewart, 1950), p. 150.

[32] *The Crooked Corridor,* p. 125.

[33] *Novels and Stories,* III, 35.

[34] "The Choice So Freely Made," p. 26.

[35] *Henry James* (New York: William Sloane Associates, 1951), p. 122.

[36] "The School of Experience in the Early Novels," *Hound and Horn,* VII (April–May, 1934), 427.

[37] "The Relativism of Henry James," *Journal of Aesthetics and Art Criticism,* XII (December, 1953), p. 239.

CHAPTER THREE

Evil in London

[1] "*The Turn of the Screw* as Poem," pp. 217, 219, 223.

[2] The governess commits the cardinal Jamesian sin of being direct. With his high regard for human dignity and privacy and corresponding aversion to the concrete "dotting of *i*'s and crossing of *t*'s," James never permits a superior character to force an issue with another person, to accuse him of a crime, or to seek a confession from him. Isabel Archer never confronts Osmond with his past; Lambert Strether never alludes to Mme. de Vionnet's adultery when speaking with her; Milly Theale never questions Densher about his relationship with Kate; and Maggie Verver uses only indirect means to learn of and then to end the adultery of the Prince and Charlotte. But the governess, and later the narrator of *The Sacred Fount,* bluntly compel others to admit their guilt.

[3] "*The Turn of the Screw* as Poem," p. 222.

[4] "The Ambiguity of Henry James," *The Question of Henry James,* p. 165.

[5] My interpretation of "The Turn of the Screw," which maintains both the reality of the ghosts and the emotional immaturity of the governess, is substantially supported by John Lydenberg, "The Governess Turns the Screws," *Nineteenth-Century Fiction,* XII (June, 1957), 37–58. For evidence that the ghosts are real, see Alexander E. Jones's excellent "Point of View in *The Turn of the Screw,*" PMLA, LXXIV (March, 1959), 112–122, which may conclude the extensive controversy initiated by Edmund Wilson's "The Ambiguity of Henry James," published in its first form in 1934.

[6] Leon Edel, "An Introductory Essay," *The Sacred Fount* (New York: Grove Press, 1953), pp. xxv–xxix, discusses the theme of depletion in the contexts of both James's earlier fiction and his personal life. Professor Edel also deals with the question of the credibility of the narrator (pp. xvi–xxv), which though highly important in itself, is not directly relevant to the present study.

[7] *The Sacred Fount,* with an introductory essay by Leon Edel, p. 45.

[8] *The Sacred Fount,* pp. 104, 128, 128–129.

[9] *The Sacred Fount,* p. 352.

[10] *American Renaissance* (New York: Oxford University Press, 1941), p. 298.

[11] *The Notebooks of Henry James,* F. O. Matthiessen and Kenneth B. Murdock, eds. (New York: Oxford University Press, 1947), p. 196.

[12] *The Art of the Novel*, p. 59.

[13] *The Art of the Novel*, p. 242.

[14] *The Letters of Henry James*, I, 124.

[15] "London," *Essays in London and Elsewhere* (New York: Harper & Bros., 1893), p. 26.

[16] *The Notebooks of Henry James*, p. 207.

[17] *The Art of the Novel*, p. 244.

[18] See Oliver Evans, "James's Air of Evil: 'The Turn of the Screw,'" *Partisan Review*, XVI (February, 1949), 185; and Joseph J. Firebaugh, "Inadequacy in Eden: Knowledge and 'The Turn of the Screw,'" *Modern Fiction Studies*, III (Spring, 1957), 60.

[19] *The Art of the Novel*, p. 123.

[20] *The Art of the Novel*, p. 105.

[21] *The Art of the Novel*, p. 147.

[22] *Selected Short Stories* by Henry James (New York: Rinehart & Co., 1950), pp. v-xiv (introduction).

[23] See Louise Dauner, "Henry James and the Garden of Death," *University of Kansas City Review*, XIX (Winter, 1952), pp. 137–143. Miss Dauner points out that James consistently uses the garden as the scene of crucial decisions and actions, so that it is alternately a garden of life (Eden) and a garden of death (Gethsemane), and at times both.

[24] *The Novels of Henry James* (New York: G. P. Putnam's Sons, 1905), p. 106.

[25] *The Sacred Fount*, p. 128.

[26] *Henry James*, p. 194.

[27] *The Sacred Fount*, pp. 135–136.

[28] *The Art of the Novel*, p. 129.

[29] See Leon Edel, "Introduction," *The Other House* (London: Rupert Hart-Davis, 1948), p. xv: "She is not a figure of unmitigated Evil—the very juxtaposition of 'bad' and 'heroine' indicates that James thought of her as possessing heroic qualities, despite her 'badness.'"

[30] *The Notebooks of Henry James*, p. 248.

[31] "*The Turn of the Screw* as Poem," p. 227; "Innocence and Evil in James's *The Turn of the Screw*," *University of Kansas City Review*, XX (Winter, 1953), 97; "James's Air of Evil: 'The Turn of the Screw,'" pp. 186–187.

[32] *The Art of the Novel*, p. 146.

[33] *The Notebooks of Henry James*, p. 178.

[34] His moral vision is somewhat offset, however, by his blindness to the intellectual genius of Mrs. Brook's circle.

[35] *The Art of the Novel*, p. 102.

[36] "Henry James, Melodramatist," *The Question of Henry James*, pp. 254–264.

[37] Characteristically, Mrs. Brook makes the perfect comment: "I'm not, as a mother—am I, Van?—bad *enough*. That's what's the matter with me. Aggie, don't you see? is the Duchess's morality, her virtue; which, by having it that way outside of you, as one may say, you can make a much better thing of. The child has been for Jane, I admit, a capital little subject, but Jane has kept her on hand and finished her like some wonderful piece of stitching. Oh as work it's of a *soigné*! There it is—to show. A woman like me has to be *herself*, poor thing, her virtue and her morality" (IX, 310–311).

[38] Even more than Nanda, Mitchy retains a high moral standard though he is outwardly the most corrupt of Mrs. Brook's set. Mrs. Brook tells Mitchy, "You're the most delicate thing I know, and it crops up with effect the oddest in the intervals of your corruption. Your talk's half the time impossible; you respect neither age nor sex nor condition; one doesn't know what you'll say or do next; and one has to return your books—*c'est tout dire*—under cover of darkness. Yet there's in the midst of all this and in the general abyss of you a little deepdown delicious niceness, a sweet sensibility, that one has actually one's self, shocked as one perpetually is at you, quite to hold one's breath and stay one's hand for fear of ruffling or bruising. There's no one in talk with whom . . . I find myself half so suddenly moved to pull up short. You've more little toes to tread on—though you pretend you haven't: I mean morally speaking, don't you know?—than even I have myself, and I've so many that I could wish most of them cut off" (IX, 85–86).

CHAPTER FOUR

Evil and the Major Phase

[1] See Christof Wegelin. *The Image of Europe in Henry James* (Dallas: Southern Methodist University Press, 1958), pp. 86–88, 189 n. 16.

[2] See *The Notebooks of Henry James*, pp. 169–174.

[3] The three novels comprise a "trilogy" in only the loosest sense of the word; though thematically and stylistically closer to each other than to any other of James's novels, *The Ambassadors, The Wings of the Dove*, and *The Golden Bowl* are totally distinct and self-contained. Other critics, however, most notably Quentin Anderson in *The American Henry James* (New Brunswick, N. J.: Rutgers University Press, 1957) have argued that the three novels form a rigid symbolical unity. Anderson's position has been ably refuted, I think, by Leon Edel in his review in *American Literature*, XXIX (January, 1958), pp. 493–495; and by Christof Wegelin, *The Image of Europe in Henry James*, pp. 184–185, n. 11.

[4] *The Letters of Henry James*, II, 104–105.

[5] *The Notebooks of Henry James*, p. 207.

[6] *The Pilgrimage of Henry James*, p. 47.

[7] Gaw is described as a bird of prey. At one point he seems to perch "like a ruffled hawk, motionless but for his single tremor, with his beak, which had pecked so many hearts out, visibly sharper than ever, yet only his talons nervous . . ." (XXV, 6).

[8] Catholic churches and monasteries frequently figure as sanctuaries from evil and anxiety, much in the same way as "the great good place" provides the author George Dane a refuge from the harassments of life. In the fullest discussion of James's treatment of Catholicism, Robert M. Slabey writes, "For James and his young American characters, the beauty and tradition of the Church attracted the person of artistic preferences; its quiet and peace offered solace for the troubled soul . . ." ("Henry James and 'The Most Impressive Convention in All History,'" *American Literature*, XXX [March, 1958], 102).

[9] Robert A. Durr, in "The Night Journey in *The Ambassadors*," *Philological Quarterly*, XXXV (January, 1956), writes that Strether has acquired

the "power to transcend the evil of antitheses by including them in a more encompassing vision . . ." (p. 29).

[10] *Henry James*, p. 245.

[11] Though written later than *The Ambassadors, The Wings of the Dove* was published slightly earlier.

[12] I am especially indebted in my discussion of *The Wings of the Dove* to R. P. Blackmur, "The Loose and Baggy Monsters of Henry James," *The Lion and the Honeycomb* (New York: Harcourt, Brace & Co., 1955), pp. 268–288; and R. W. B. Lewis, "The Vision of Grace: James's 'The Wings of the Dove,' " *Modern Fiction Studies*, III (Spring, 1957), 33–40.

[13] *The Art of the Novel*, p. 164.

[14] America is less an operative force in *The Wings* than in *The Ambassadors* and *The Golden Bowl*. However, what James says in his preface about Milly's nationality deserves comment: he speaks of there being "fifty reasons for her national and social status. She should be the last fine flower . . . of an 'old' New York stem . . ." (*The Art of the Novel*, p. 292). In Milly, James is invoking the memory not only of Minny Temple, but also of the New York of his youth, which as his late fiction (for example, "A Round of Visits" and *The Ivory Tower*) makes abundantly clear, has lost its charm and innocence. To James's mind materialism and vulgarity have corrupted America as well as England, so that in the world of *The Wings of the Dove* only an anachronism will serve James as a suitable tragic victim, for the moral attributes which James required of his heroine he could no longer detect in Anglo-American culture.

[15] See Quentin Anderson, *The American Henry James*, pp. 246–247, for additional instances in which the merchandising attitude dominates human affairs.

[16] See Ernest Sandeen, "*The Wings of the Dove* and *The Portrait of a Lady*: A Study of James's Later Phase," *PMLA*, LXIX (December, 1954), pp. 1066–1070.

[17] *The Destructive Element* (London: Jonathan Cape, 1953), p. 67.

[18] *The Art of the Novel*, p. 293.

[19] Jean Kimball, "The Abyss and the Wings of the Dove: The Image as a Revelation," *Nineteenth-Century Fiction*, X (March, 1956), 281–300, discusses the meaning and importance of the "abyss" image in *The Wings of the Dove*. Miss Kimball, however, sees the image only in its relation to Milly Theale's predicament.

Frederick C. Crews, *The Tragedy of Manners: Moral Drama in the Later Novels of Henry James* (New Haven: Yale University Press, 1957), p. 72, calls attention to the recurrent water images, which, in my view, supplement the abyss images.

[20] Especially in *The Wings of the Dove*, James's treatment of the past invites comparison with the "heap of broken images" theme in the poetry of T. S. Eliot.

[21] Morton Dauwen Zabel, *Craft and Character in Modern Fiction*, pp. 280–281.

[22] In recent years a critical controversy has risen over James's attitude to- wards the Ververs. F. R. Leavis (*The Great Tradition*, pp. 159–161) and F. O. Matthiessen (*Henry James: The Major Phase* [New York: Oxford University Press, 1944], pp. 92–93) find it a weakness in the novel that James seems unaware of certain objectionable traits in them, mainly their

consideration of their marriage partners simply as "pieces" for the elder Verver's collection, and their refusal to view their marriages as anything other than noble deeds enacted for the sake of each other.

Other critics, however, have demonstrated that James's attitude towards the Ververs is definitely critical and ironical. See, for example: Joseph J. Firebaugh, "The Ververs," *Essays in Criticism*, IV (October, 1954), 400–410; Francis Fergusson, "The Drama in *The Golden Bowl*," *Hound and Horn*, VII (April–May, 1934), 407–413; and Christof Wegelin, *The Image of Europe in Henry James*, pp. 122–140.

²³ "Introduction," *The Golden Bowl* (New York: Grove Press, 1952), p. vi.

²⁴ *The American Novel: 1789–1939* (New York: Macmillan Co., 1940), p. 184.

²⁵ "Myth and Dialectic in the Later Novels," *Kenyon Review*, V (Autumn, 1943), 565.

²⁶ "*The Golden Bowl* Revisited," *Sewanee Review*, LXIII (Winter, 1955), 21.

²⁷ "*The Golden Bowl* Revisited," p. 23.

²⁸ "Henry James's World of Images," *PMLA*, LXVIII (December, 1953), 956.

²⁹ *Henry James*, p. 267.

CHAPTER FIVE

The Last Tales: The Appalled Appalling

¹ *A Small Boy and Others*, p. 348.

² *The Finer Grain* (London: Methuen & Co., 1910), p. 153.

³ *The Finer Grain*, p. 171.

⁴ F. O. Matthiessen, *Henry James: The Major Phase*, p. 117, writes that Winch "had penetrated into a world so corrupted by money that the only escape seemed to be by violence." It seems clear, however, that the public offense of materialism is not so much the reason for Winch's suicide as the private offense of betrayal—the major sin in James's work.

⁵ *The Finer Grain*, p. 233.

⁶ *The Finer Grain*, p. 238.

⁷ *The Finer Grain*, pp. 261, 259.

⁸ *The Finer Grain*, p. 307.

⁹ See Edwin Fussell, "Hawthorne, James and 'The Common Doom,'" *American Quarterly*, X (Winter, 1958), 438–453, for a discussion of this aspect of James's work.

¹⁰ Charles G. Hoffmann, *The Shorter Novels of Henry James* (New York: Bookman Associates, 1957), pp. 114–115, briefly discusses the element of fate in "The Bench of Desolation." Kate's comment, "Of course you've suffered . . . you inevitably had to! We have to . . . to do or to be or to get anything" (*The Finer Grain*, p. 279), suggests a limited but significant concept of fate: suffering is inevitable in the world, but it is a kind of inverted grace (as in the novels of Mauriac and Greene), providing a condition of consciousness hostile to egotism and necessary for spiritual growth. The will is free, however, to accept or reject the grace.

It is interesting to compare the treatment of suffering in "The Bench of

Desolation" with that in works by Melville, Hawthorne, and Faulkner. In James, suffering almost always purifies. In Melville, however, especially in "Benito Cereno" and "Bartleby," suffering overwhelms consciousness and leads to total withdrawal from the world. In Hawthorne, most notably in "Young Goodman Brown," exposure to evil can easily intensify spiritual pride. The same is frequently true in Faulkner, many of whose characters become increasingly withdrawn from the world and ego-centered through suffering.

[11] *The Finer Grain,* pp. 245, 232, 232.

[12] *The Finer Grain,* p. 242.

[13] James is explicit on this point: "My hero's adventure [in "The Jolly Corner"] takes the form so to speak of his turning the tables, as I think I called it, on a 'ghost' or whatever, a visiting or haunting apparition other-wise qualified to appal *him;* and thereby winning a sort of victory by the appearance, and the evidence, that this personage or presence was more overwhelmingly affected by him than he by it" (*The Notebooks of Henry James,* pp. 367–368).

Leon Edel, in quoting this passage, calls it "a curiously inaccurate account of the story [James] had written. The novelist here substitutes the night-mare for the story. In the story the hero does not appal the ghost, but is ap-palled and overwhelmed by it" (*Henry James: The Untried Years* [Phila-delphia and New York: J. B. Lippincott Co., 1953], p. 75). Certainly the issue is ambiguous: the motives and feelings Brydon attributes to the ghost are often questionable. It is clear that until his final night in the house Brydon is the pursuer and the ghost is the pursued: "Who had ever before so turned the tables and become himself, in the apparitional world, an incal-culable terror?" (XVII, 451). Brydon becomes frightened only when he believes that the alter ego has entered a particular room in the upper rear of the house; then Brydon descends the stairs in terror. However, at the foot of the stairs he sees the presence, its hands covering its face. At this point Brydon advances; the ghost retreats. The ghost then removes his hands to reveal his hideous face, and Brydon faints. Clearly there is at least a mutual terror. Also it is conceivable that the ghost covers his face not to prevent Brydon from seeing him, but to prevent himself from seeing Brydon. See, in this connection, Floyd Stovall's interesting interpretation, "Henry James's 'The Jolly Corner,'" *Nineteenth-Century Fiction,* XII (June, 1957), 72–84.

CONCLUSION

[1] *The Destructive Element,* p. 67.

[2] "Attitudes toward Henry James," *The Question of Henry James,* p. 278.

[3] *The Art of the Novel,* pp. 45–46.

Index

A NOTE ABOUT THE AUTHOR

JOSEPH ANTHONY WARD, JR. was born in Baltimore, Maryland, in 1931. He received his A.B. degree *cum laude* from the University of Notre Dame in 1952 and his M.A. and Ph.D. from Tulane University (1954, 1957). From 1953 to 1957 he served as a graduate assistant and instructor in English at Tulane, and in 1957 joined the faculty of Southwestern Louisiana University as an assistant professor. He was awarded a Guggenheim fellowship for 1960–1961 for study of Henry James's conception of structure in the novel. Although THE IMAGINATION OF DISASTER is his first book, Professor Ward has contributed articles to a dozen scholarly periodicals, among them *American Literature*, the *Journal of English and Germanic Philology*, *Criticism*, the *Western Humanities Review*, *Nineteenth-Century Fiction*, and *Names*.

Professor Ward is married and has two daughters.